From Habits to Social Structures

Studies in Sociology: Symbols, Theory and Society

Edited by Elżbieta Hałas and Risto Heiskala

Vol. 7

PETER LANG

Frankfurt am Main · Berlin · Bern · Bruxelles · New York · Oxford · Wien

Antti Gronow

From Habits to Social Structures

Pragmatism and Contemporary Social Theory

PETER LANG
Internationaler Verlag der Wissenschaften

Bibliographic Information published by the Deutsche Nationalbibliothek
The Deutsche Nationalbibliothek lists this publication in the Deutsche Nationalbibliografie; detailed bibliographic data is available in the internet at http://dnb.d-nb.de.

Copy editor: Kimmo Aaltonen

ISSN 1618-775X
ISBN 978-3-631-61574-4
© Peter Lang GmbH
Internationaler Verlag der Wissenschaften
Frankfurt am Main 2011
All rights reserved.

All parts of this publication are protected by copyright. Any utilisation outside the strict limits of the copyright law, without the permission of the publisher, is forbidden and liable to prosecution. This applies in particular to reproductions, translations, microfilming, and storage and processing in electronic retrieval systems.

www.peterlang.de

Contents

Acknowledgements	7
1 Introduction: Grounds for Pragmatism	9
Action and Social Structures	11
Pragmatism: A Very Brief History	13
How Many Pragmatisms?	15
Unnecessary Representations?	19
Language, Meaning and Evolution	25
Pragmatism and Science	28
The Concept of Habit	30
A Note on Pragmatist Literature	35
Mead and Intersubjectivity	36
Institutionalization as Habitualization	45
Habitus and Habits	53
Pragmatism and Social Philosophy	60
2 The Over- or the Undersocialized Conception of Man?	
Practice Theory and the Problem of Intersubjectivity	69
Practice and Sociality	71
Exit Introspection, Enter Reflexivity	74
Internal Conversation, Social Structures, and Habitual Action	78
Conclusion	81

3 Not by Rules or Choice Alone: A Pragmatist Critique of Institution
  Theories in Economics and Sociology   83
    Regulative Institutionalism   85
    Normative Institutionalism   87
    Discursive Institutionalism   89
    Habitual Institutionalism   92
    Conclusion   99

4 Uneasy Bedfellows or Natural Allies? Bourdieu and Pragmatism   103
    Bourdieu in Context   105
    Converging on Habituality   107
    Points of Contention: Creativity and Identity   112
    Where Does this Leave Us?   116

5 Integrating the Capabilities Approach with Pragmatism   121
    Beyond the GNP: Capabilities and Freedom   122
    Actors: Passive and Active   124
    The Issue of Relativism   125
    Capabilities and the Role of the Public   128
    Conclusion   130

6 The Road Ahead   131

  References   135

  Index   147

Acknowledgements

Despite the name, the social sciences are not always the most social of scientific and scholarly disciplines. One can sit in one's chamber (possibly even in the infamous ivory tower), contemplate social issues, and write articles and books by oneself. Such a lonesome enterprise is probably the fate of some researchers in the field of social sciences and, especially, in social theory. However, I have had the privilege and the opportunity to be in contact and collaboration with a host of inspiring and helpful people. Risto Heiskala drew my attention to the interesting interdisciplinary discussions on the nature of institutions. This attention eventually paid off as it was the topic of my master's thesis. Risto was also kind enough to act as a supervisor of my doctoral thesis, which you are now holding in your hands. I am immensely grateful to Risto for all his words of advice and encouragement. While Risto is responsible for bringing institutional theories to my attention – which eventually led into an interest in pragmatism – Erkki Kilpinen, the other supervisor of my thesis, is to be thanked for guiding me in the maze of pragmatism. Erkki has been an indispensable help because of his immense expertise in pragmatist social theory. The comments and critiques of the pre-examiners of this thesis, Neil Gross and Seppo Raiski, definitely made it a better book. Elżbieta Hałas, the editor of the book series *Studies in Sociology: Symbols, Theory and Society*, has been very helpful with her comments and suggestions.

Arto Noro, the grey eminence of social theory in Finland, was the first teacher who succeeded in making social theory interesting and alive for me. Therefore I wish to thank him for the inspiration and education he gave through his lectures, the post-graduate seminar – and sessions in the local pub. There are also other teachers who made the post-graduate seminar interesting and worthwhile: Risto Alapuro, Risto Eräsaari, Riitta Jallinoja and Anssi Peräkylä. While writing this book, I had the opportunity to work at the Department of Sociology (nowadays part of a bigger Department of Social Research), University of Helsinki. I shared an office with Anu Katainen and thank her for all her help – and for all the laughs. There are many people at the department I wish to thank but I will mention the following: Tapani Alkula, Elina Haavio-Mannila, Kimmo Herttua, Tuukka Kaidesoja, Kaisa Ketokivi, Pekka Kosonen, Riikka Kotanen, Turo-Kimmo Lehtonen, Eeva Luhtakallio, Kati Mustala, Aino Sinnemäki, Pekka Sulkunen, Teemu Turunen, Mikko Virtanen and Suvi-Tuuli Waltari. The former Depertment of Social Policy, which is nowadays part of the Department of Social Research, has its share of fine minds. Of these, I thank Keijo Rahkonen and, especially, Semi Purhonen, for their company at lunch, in conference excursions and in the local pub.

The study group known as the "Sunday Circle" (*Sunnuntaipiiri* in Finnish) has been an unofficial intellectual reference group throughout my graduate and post-graduate studies. Many of the ideas found in this book were discussed with Esa Mäkinen, Sampo Villanen, Heikki Wilenius, Anna Ylä-Anttila, Tuomas Ylä-Anttila and the former members of this group. I am grateful for having such intelligent friends! There are also intelligent pragmatists in Helsinki. These pragmatists, mostly philosophers, tend to meet at the "Metaphysical Club," and I owe thanks to all the members of this club for their educative discussions. Alfred Kordelin Foundation, Kone Foundation and the Academy of Finland have provided financial support enabling my research. My parents, Jukka Gronow and Terttu Luukkonen, have always encouraged my studies and been helpful in so many ways. Last but not least, I thank Jaana Markkula for all her patience and love.

January 2011, Helsinki
Antti Gronow

CHAPTER 1

Introduction: Grounds for Pragmatism

Pragmatism is a word that should by now be familiar to many social scientists, at least to researchers working in the field of social theory. This word also often comes up in political contexts. For example, a recent book on President Barack Obama's political outlook argues that the "close connection between the philosophy of pragmatism and the culture of democratic decision making illuminates crucial dimensions of Obama's thinking" (Kloppenberg 2011, xii). However, when one goes through the trouble of looking into the meaning of the word "pragmatism," one finds confusion: it seems to mean different things to different people. One of the intentions of this book is to bring some sense into this confusion. For example, pragmatism has sometimes been taken as a catchphrase for epistemological stances in which "anything goes." However, other authors argue that the real novelty and contribution of this tradition has to do with its view of action as the context in which all things human take place. Thus it is action rather than, for example, knowledge that should be our starting point in social theory. Furthermore, explanations for enduring social aspects, such as social structures, should always be related to action (though not necessarily reduced to it). This line of arguing has been put forward by Hans Joas, for example, most famously in his book *The Creativity of Action* (1996). The framework of my study is also in this action-centered approach.

In what follows, I present the various lines of reasoning within pragmatism and its general relevance for social theory. There is plenty of literature focusing on pragmatism but concise presentations are lacking, especially in social theory. Furthermore, few authors have pondered on substantial issues of social theory with the help of pragmatism. My focus is especially on G. H. Mead and John Dewey because these authors are undoubtedly the most important classical pragmatists for social theory. However, despite their names being well-known their arguments have often been misunderstood. The introductory section of the book situates pragmatism within the context of social theory. Some of the discussion will be on a fairly abstract level. For example, I will discuss the issues of representation and meaning. However, this introductory section will also contextualize the main core of the book, which consists of four chapters.[1] These chapters deal with more substantial issues of social theory; they all take their cue from the issue of the relationship between action and social structures but they do so from different perspectives. The more abstract discussion hopefully paves the way for these substantial themes. Thus, I approach the relevance of pragmatism from different angles – all of which are united by the argument that a consideration of habituality is important in explaining the relationship between action and social structures.

Too often it is the case in social theory that action and social structures appear as opposing entities. The concept of habit offers a way out of this confrontational dilemma. Habitual action is the major explanation for the emergence of social structures. Action produces structures and their *re*production takes place when action is habitualized; that is, when we develop the disposition to act in a certain manner in familiar environments. These environments are always more or less social (consisting of other actors). Each chapter will highlight this general insight but from different angles. The more specific themes have to do with intersubjectivity, the nature of institutions, the differences and similarities between Pierre Bourdieu and pragmatism, and the role of the social context in promoting freedom of action. Thus the underlying argument is that some of the problems related to these four substantial and contemporary issues are such that pragmatism can offer novel solutions.

Pragmatism has experienced a small renaissance in both social theory and philosophy in recent years. It is a renaissance in the sense that pragmatism was influential in these disciplines at the beginning of the twentieth century, especially in the United States. This heyday was followed by a decline which can be dated to the 1940s and 1950s. Gross (2002, 56) has elaborated on the possible reasons for this decline in the following way: "the academic environment was transformed by the influence of psychoanalysis, existentialism, structuralism, analytic philosophy, and functionalism, and was reeling from the horrors of fascism and the shock entry into the atomic age." For example, some authors argued that pragmatism was a form of behaviorism and had to be discarded because behaviorism is not capable of dealing with voluntary aspects of action. In addition, many Europeans saw pragmatism as an apologia for American capitalism and entrepreneurship. However, these accusations were not accurate characterizations of classical pragmatism.

The recent renaissance of pragmatism has a lot to do with Richard Rorty. Opinions differ regarding the contribution he made to the pragmatist heritage but

---

1 Two of these four chapters have been published in journals and one in an edited book.

one thing certain: without his influence, pragmatism would probably be less known than it is today, both in professional circles and also in the public arena. It is also undeniable that Rorty has a direct link with pragmatism on the level of ideas even though this has sometimes been disputed. However, as I argue later on, this link is blurred by the fact that he tends to exaggerate certain features of pragmatism at the expense of other, equally important, aspects.

The philosophical foundations of pragmatism – although many pragmatists are not happy with the expression *foundations* – are undoubtedly laid down in the thought of Charles S. Peirce. The fragmentary nature of Peirce's *oeuvre* and the complexity of some aspects of his thought have sometimes prevented people from seeing the common themes of pragmatism starting with Peirce's work. My study is about the habitual nature of action which is a theme that starts with Peirce and runs through classical pragmatism. However, I am not trying to show how this theme penetrates classical pragmatism, as this has already been demonstrated (see, e.g., Kilpinen 2000). Instead, I will be building on these previous arguments.

Action and Social Structures

The substantial problem of my study deals with action and social theory. More specifically, it has to do with the relation between action and social structures. Their relationship is an age-old issue and one could argue that it constitutes the hard core of social theory. Sometimes it is argued, or implicitly assumed, that theories of social structures are alternatives to theories of action. Thus, because it is structures that "do the talking," no attention need be paid to action or only in passing. Quite often one also encounters this argument as its mirror image so that theories of action are thought to be reducible to theories of structures. These two lines of reasoning have often been called methodological holism and methodological individualism, respectively. However, in their extreme forms they can easily be called into question. For example, Joas argues as follows:

> The theory of action does not per se compete with the theory of social order. (…) In fact, the theory of action directly compels us to pose the problem of social order. *Every theory of action entails theoretical assumptions about the nature of the social order that implicitly or explicitly corresponds to it.* (Joas 1993, 135, emphasis added.)

In the above citation Joas mentions theories of social order. These theories discuss the process through which action leads to social formations with relative stability. Once these formations are stable enough, one can call them social structures. Thus, for all practical purposes we can discuss theories of social order in the same breath as theories of social structures.² Theories of action and theories of structures (or social order, as Joas calls them) are two sides of the same coin. It is not an arbitrary issue what the other side of the coin looks like; it is dependent on the particular theory on the "other side of the coin." Even a holistic theory implicitly assumes a theory of action, in this case a theory in which action is determined and dictated by social structures. Of course, in practice such holism amounts to the disappearance of action as structures dictate our every move but, nonetheless, this is a theory of action (albeit with little room left for proper agency). Thus, it is not only that theories of action entail a theory about social order, as Joas said above, but also that theories of social order or social structures necessarily entail theories of action: what one says about action entails implicit or explicit assumptions about structures – and *vice versa*. Naturally, one does not always have to deal with both issues, those having to do with action and those with structures, at the same time. However, this is precisely what I intend to do. My central claim is that pragmatism has an action-centered focus which never loses sight of structures. This is due to the importance of the concept of habit in pragmatism; habit is a general category of action but it is also an explanation for the way in which social structures come into existence. This does not mean that action and structures would be the same thing because both have properties that the other one lacks. For example, proper intentions are present in action but they are lacking in the case of structures.³

When it comes to theories of action and social structures, it is often recognized that pragmatism is capable of avoiding some of the pitfalls of other theoretical approaches. For example, Shilling (2008, 3) argues that "pragmatism's recognition and explorations of the distinctive properties of, and the dynamic relationship that exists between, the external and internal environments of human action can help avoid the dangers of conflation." By conflation is meant a reductive explanation, in this case either into social structures or into our inner "environments." For example, if it is claimed that addiction is solely explained by the genes that one happens to have, then this is a reduction in the latter sense. One can also use this expression in the case of theories that conflate social explanations into purely individual acts (so-called methodological individualism). Margaret Archer has used the terms downwards and upwards conflation to analyze the two ways in which a reduction can be done. In her own words:

---

2 The idea of social order is often used as an antithesis to situations of conflict. Thus, there are theories of social order which compete with conflict theories. The theme of social competition and conflicts will be discussed later in relation to Pierre Bourdieu's thought.

3 Of course, one could argue that in the case of social movements, for example, structures can have intention-like qualities. However, this can never be literally true even if it made sense in a metaphorical way (as in intention-*like* qualities).

> Downwards conflation means that the properties of "people" can be "upwardly reduced" to properties of the system, which alone has causal powers. Upwards conflation means that the properties of the "parts" can be "downwardly reduced" to properties of the "people," who alone have causal powers (Archer 2000, 5).

It can be claimed that pragmatism is a theory which is guilty of neither of these forms of reductionism. Rather, pragmatists often argue that structures do indeed depend on action, on habitualized action, but one cannot reduce all structural properties to purely individual acts. Thus, if one were to enquire into why social theorists should be interested in pragmatism, the answer would no doubt refer to the fruitful and novel way of theorizing the relationship between action and structures.

The history of sociology is frequently presented as a narrative in which sociology is a reaction against utilitarian conceptions of social order. For example, the starting point of Talcott Parsons thought was the observation that purely utilitarian actors will never maintain a stable social order. Therefore Parsons' own solution to this dilemma was that normative institutions are needed to ensure stability. Thus, Parsonian sociology attacks utilitarian thought on the grounds of social order. Kilpinen (2000) argues that pragmatism attacked utilitarianism on this ground as well but it also criticizes the utilitarian stance on action and social order. Joas (1993) has also made the argument that pragmatism is critical of the utilitarian view on action and consciousness which maintains that consciousness is about calculative operations towards some pre-given ends. Joas tends to see this critique as pragmatism's only line of attack.[4] On closer inspection, however, it turns out that Joas is probably of the same view as Kilpinen; in my interpretation Joas sees the problem of action and consciousness as so fundamental that it also undermines utilitarian conceptions of social order. Both authors agree that the starting point should be habituality which occasionally gets interrupted by conflicting stimuli originating in our inner and outer environments. The order of things is not therefore that of consciousness preceding action but quite the opposite: action precedes consciousness – or, to be more precise, action incorporates consciousness.

Pragmatism: A Very Brief History

Baert and Turner (2007, 11) have argued that pragmatism "can be seen as a response to the consequences of the Civil War, which was seen by the pragmatists as a failure of democratic culture." This is probably an apt conclusion. However, I would also add that just as important as the Civil War might have been, behind pragma-

---

4 Later on, Joas has argued with Knöbl that for pragmatists "it was the *connection between action and consciousness*, rather than that between action and order, that stood centre stage" (Joas and Knöbl 2009, 125). This is probably an apt characterization.

tism there is also a revolution in ideas brought about by Charles Darwin. All the classical pragmatists dealt with the question of how philosophy should be reformed after the Darwinian revolution. This Darwinian impact was of such magnitude that John Dewey has been called "evolution's first philosopher" (see Popp 2007). However, this epithet could be added to any one of the classical pragmatists. One of the main conclusions that they drew from Darwinism, as will be explained in the course of this book, was that action is the context of all things human (and all things *alive* to be more precise).

In a nutshell, the history of pragmatism goes like this: Peirce is the founding figure with his pragmatist maxim which states that beliefs are to be judged by their practical consequences. Thus, Peirce sets the ball rolling and William James is the first one to pick it up. However, some interpretations of pragmatism upset Peirce so much that he renamed his own doctrine "pragmaticism," reserving this epithet especially for the study of meaning (Kilpinen 2000, 35). Eventually John Dewey and George Herbert Mead, among others, catch up with the rising tide of pragmatism. However, Peirce's reception was made difficult by the fact that he did not publish a systematic discussion of his ideas and did not receive full credit for the originality of his thought in his lifetime. As Kilpinen (ibid., 41) states, "he is famous for his temptation to plan overambitious projects whose fulfillment was beyond any mortal man's powers." This meant that Dewey, in his time, was greatly influenced by Peirce. James, for his part, was mostly responsible for the impression that pragmatism is about wishful thinking. As argued by Margolis (2006, 7) "James was more than tempted to take the 'good' of *believing* this or that to be (at least at times) sufficient grounds for counting it *ipso facto* true." However, if this good is taken to include all the results of the belief in question, then it need not have anything to do with such idealism. Nevertheless, there is a strand of pragmatism emanating in James' thought which finds it difficult to conceptually separate evidence from wishful thinking (it can be seen, for example, in an interest in the philosophy of religion).

As is well known, James' main interests were in the field of psychology. Peirce, the inventor of pragmatism, has, in turn, sometimes been taken as a "mere" logician and a forerunner of logical positivism; these interpretations usually go hand in hand. He was certainly a logician but his concept of logic is different from a contemporary one. In his hands, inferences are always related to action and this also means that logic is not merely a formal exercise (see Kilpinen 2000). Peirce's logic is based on semiotics, that is, on the study of how action becomes meaningful. A general overview of his oeuvre is beyond the scope of my study due to its multi-faceted and philosophical nature (see, for example, Bergman 2004). In addition to Darwinism, which will be discussed later, pragmatists were also influenced by Hegel. This is especially true of Dewey and Mead, who started their philosophical careers as Hegelians. However, both eventually turned towards naturalism in which there is no place for an overarching and idealistic *Geist*. However, some traces of Hegelianism remained in their thinking. For example, Mead (1936, 135) admitted that "Hegel is correct in the assumption that the development of our knowledge takes place through conflict." Thus, its development, and also the development of mind, is a process.

How Many Pragmatisms?

It is often overlooked that there are in fact different varieties of pragmatism, although they are all supposedly covered by this label. Thus, it should be acknowledged that there are so many components and views of pragmatism that it is impossible to discuss all of pragmatism as a theory (although there is a pragmatist theory of action). This diversity can cause such amazement that one might even begin to wonder "whether the label serves any real purpose" (Haack 2004, 5). However, this diversity can serve pedagogical purposes. As Richard Bernstein (1992, 824) has argued, "we must be careful not to underestimate the heterogeneity, diversity, and sharp internal conflicts which have always characterized the pragmatists." This is because these conflicts can teach us as much as the issues on which consensus has been reached. For some commentators this discussion of the internal conflicts of pragmatism can seem boring or even schizophrenic.[5] Indeed, there is the danger of getting stuck in fruitless debates on the proper reason to label someone a pragmatist. For example, the frequently asked question whether Richard Rorty was truly a pragmatist is an endless debate and it is not interesting in itself. However, the question of the nature of pragmatism is not only a question of names and labels – but of ideas. That is, it tells us something about how, for example, truth should be understood.

Misak (2007, 2) has proposed that what she calls "new pragmatism" shares two postulates (as opposed to Rorty's "neopragmatism"). The first pillar is that "standards of objectivity come into being and evolve over time, but that being historically situated in this way does not detract from their objectivity." Thus, it differs from Foucauldian genealogy, for example, which usually contains the supposition – either explicit or implicit – that showing the historicity of some idea implies that it is not truly objective and therefore no true objectivity exists. Peirce's starting point was the insight that Cartesian doubt is empty – it is doubt on paper which is impossible in reality because one cannot doubt all of one's beliefs at the same time. What needs to be done is to situate doubt in concrete action situations, in the crisis of our habits. This means that only some of our habits are usually in doubt at the same time and the other habits, those not in doubt, are the background which enable reflection.

---

5 This is, for example, the impression that a recent reviewer of a Finnish book on pragmatism conveys to his readers (see Ylikoski 2009).

As James (1975, 35) argues, "[t]he most violent revolutions in an individual's beliefs leave most of his old order standing." Thus, concrete action situations and the problems encountered during the course of action are the reason why doubt arises. This also means that the formation of beliefs and habits is related to problem-solving activity. Problem-solving does not necessarily refer to explicit puzzles and such, but to all situations where the social or material environment causes us to reflect on our habits. Furthermore, this is also an explanation for the phenomenon of consciousness; it arises, as a part of action processes, in situations where there are contradictory responses towards our environment. As a theory of consciousness, it could be labeled a contradiction theory (see Gillespie 2005).[6]

The second of Misak's pillars of pragmatism states that knowledge has no certain foundations. This statement is definitely a central part of pragmatism from its very beginnings. Thus, we can never be certain that our present beliefs and habits rest on solid, infallible foundations. There can always be new situations of doubt facing us and in these situations one should not cling on to old beliefs just for the sake of routine-like habituality. All this can sound quite philosophical, but discussions about the role of crises in our habits not need to be abstract. It is possible to frame the pragmatist agenda in research within actual crises in daily life. For example, Ketokivi (2008) has used a Meadian framework in her analysis of the way in which the reorganization of family relationships can act as a biographical disruption and a "wound" of selfhood.

To quote Bernstein (1992, 832) again: "A tradition lives when it is not simply honored or embalmed but when it is constantly reinterpreted and provides new sources of inspiration." A debate on who is a pragmatist and, more importantly, what pragmatism *is*, can certainly contribute to such a continuous reinterpretation. There probably is a danger of "patronizing" the classical pragmatists, but this danger can be avoided by critically drawing on their work in tackling, for example, the issues of "sociality, intersubjectivity, communication, and practical rationality" (ibid., 835). These issues are all of concern for pragmatists but I think that our general attitude towards classical pragmatists – or towards all classical authors for that matter – should be one of critically drawing on their work in tackling *contemporary problems*. This is precisely my purpose: to discuss contemporary social theory with the help of ideas from classical pragmatism.

When discussing classical pragmatists, it should be remembered that they were first and foremost philosophers, not sociologists. However, both pragmatist philosophy and pragmatist sociology share a basic understanding of action and its self-correc-

---

6 Gillespie (2005) also distinguishes other theories of consciousness. He rightly reminds us that a theory of *selfhood* needs the Meadian social component and thus a mere contradiction theory of consciousness is not enough. However, I think it is still safe to say that a contradiction theory of consciousness is one that is shared by all classical pragmatists – an issue not properly discussed by Gillespie.

tive rationality (in situations of doubt) (Kilpinen 2000, 37). As Gross (2009, 366) argues, "the classical pragmatists were for the most part united in their understanding of the basic nature of human activity vis-à-vis the social and natural worlds." It is human activity or action that lies at the heart of pragmatism and, as Gross' words suggest, classical pragmatists also had an understanding of the importance of social relations for our activity. The issue of self-corrective rationality refers to the way in which rationality is about reflecting on one's reactions to environmental stimuli – and about correcting one's reactions if need be. Naturally some pragmatists had more to say about the role of sociality and society than others, and without doubt one can say that G. H. Mead and John Dewey are the foremost figures in this regard. Mead developed a sophisticated conception of the social nature of selfhood, whereas Dewey touched upon almost all imaginable topics under the rubric of social science.

Pragmatism and sociology have had an uneasy relationship. Easily viewed as purely an American enterprise, pragmatism has often been met with a shrug in European countries. However, there are famous exceptions. Èmile Durkheim, one of the undisputed fathers of sociology, found pragmatism a challenge to the tradition of rationalism that has dominated Western thought. According to him, the acceptance of "the form of irrationalism represented by pragmatism" would mean that "the whole French mind would have to be radically changed" (Durkheim 1983, 1).[7] He also argued that pragmatism "claims to explain truth psychologically and subjectively" (ibid., 67). Durkheim saw pragmatism as being a representative of utilitarian thought as it presumably derives truth from mere psychological satisfaction.

It is easy to point out that this is a crude caricature of most forms of pragmatism. As Joas (1993, 59-60) argues, "pragmatism is above all a reflection on the fact that the subject is embedded in praxis and sociality prior to any form of conscious intentionality of action." Thus, our embedding in practical and social relations is the main focus here, not explaining truth psychologically and subjectively. Truth is not about mere psychological satisfaction but rather about facing up to problems of action in all of their social and material facets. Furthermore, Durkheim characterized pragmatism as a monism of action, that is, as a denial of conscious rationality. According to Joas, this characterization fits behaviorism better than pragmatism. Indeed, pragmatism has never denied that there is a place for conscious, reflexive thought. As Veblen (1898, 188) argued, "man mentally digests the content of the habits under whose guidance he acts." Joas (2008, 46) himself is interested in a fine-grained analysis of the phenomenon of articulating our experiences, as this citation shows: "we should not simply speak of an interplay between the experiences and articulation but rather of an interplay among the situation experienced, our pre-reflective experience, our in-

---

7 Durkheim's book on pragmatism was published posthumously and is based on lecture notes taken by his students.

dividual articulation, and the cultural repertoire of interpretative patterns." To come back to Durkheim, his argument rests on "the false Cartesian alternative of action as purely physical movement versus thought as a purely mental construct" (Joas 1993, 71). We can therefore tentatively conclude that Durkheim is so enmeshed in dualistic thinking that he fails to grasp the arguments of pragmatism. Thus, if one is not willing to let go of the pre-Darwinian idea that the body is what acts in a material world and the mind is entirely on a plane of its own (unaffected by "crude" causality) then it is impossible to understand the arguments of pragmatists.

The main avenues of pragmatist thought in American sociology were the so-called Chicago School and symbolic interactionism. To be more precise, symbolic interactionism can be read as the continuation of the Chicago School of sociology. The groundwork for this school – exhibited in the work of names like William I. Thomas, Florian Znaniecki and Robert Park – was laid down by the work of Mead and, especially, by Dewey. Shilling (2008, 28-29) has argued that the Chicago School inherited from pragmatism a concern for both the external and internal environments of action. The external environment was mainly the modern city, whereas the interest in the internal "environment" had to do with taking note of individual factors besides social ones. This contrasts, for instance, with Durkheim's famous dictum that the social should be explained with the social.

Symbolic interactionism, a movement founded by Mead's former student Herbert Blumer, built on these foundations but it did so quite selectively. As its name implies, symbolic interactionists were fond of claiming that action is mediated by symbols. Thus, it is not a procedure of mechanical reaction. Deweyan pragmatism stressed that stimuli usually do not elicit mechanical responses because what counts as a stimuli is dependent on preceding action, that is, what we happen to be doing. The duration of action processes can vary from a very short time period to an entire lifetime. For example, writing a dissertation is an action process that usually takes a few years. Naturally most action processes are not as clearly defined as in this example. Mead made an important suggestion about the central role of symbolic thought in human action. However, symbolic interactionists sometimes tended to forget the grounding of symbols *in* action. This forgetfulness is partly explained by the fact that these sociologists – as one might guess – concentrate on interactions between people and not on action as such. According to Joas and Knöbl (2009, 136), symbolic interactionists quite rightly "conceive of 'society' as a process of action, rather than a structure or a system, because this [the latter view] problematically implies that social relations are fixed." However, this has led to the "the profound radicalization of Mead's insight into the fundamentally processual and never-ending nature of identity formation, characteristic of some postmodern writings, [which] has generated untenable exaggerations" (ibid., 147). Untenable exaggerations can follow if the habitual side of things is downplayed; for example, in Dewey's thought, habits are the mechanism which guarantees continuity of character. All in all, one can agree with Joas (1993, 17) that "the Chicago School (…) was itself only a partial realization – from the theoretical standpoint – of the possibilities inherent in the social philosophy of pragmatism."

The possible affiliation of pragmatism with so-called postmodernist thought is an issue that has occasionally arisen. One of the main themes of postmodern discussions has been a critique of crude binary oppositions. This theme is undoubtedly shared by many pragmatists. For example, for Dewey the distinction between subjective and objective aspects is one of relations, not of absolutes. It is easy to agree with Bernstein (1992, 837) when he argues that "many 'postmodern' thinkers slip back into the crude form of binary thinking when they damn universality, identity, totality, and praise particularity, difference, fragmentation." This is self-contradictory and self-defeating because we have to have some rational principles if we are to have any enquiries in the first place. The other option is remaining silent – or idealizing poetry and/or madness. Pragmatists have usually argued that rationality, which is basically the ability to critically reflect upon one's habits, is not infallible. However, this does not mean that we should just throw up our hands and give up trying. What it *does* mean is that we have to learn from our mistakes. Formulating a new belief, and segmenting it as a habit, then, does not guarantee that we get it right this time. Furthermore, what getting it "right" means depends on the environment. Social habits are not necessarily false or mistaken in the sense that more straightforward and simpler beliefs can be. When one looks at a particular social habit from a sociological perspective, then the important thing is to dissect the way in which it is related to other habits in the community in question.

Unnecessary Representations?

As mentioned, Rorty has a controversial position within pragmatism but it is still safe to say that "Rorty's pragmatist lineage, particularly from Dewey, is in important respects uncontestable" (Westbrook 2005, 145 n17). Thus Rorty's thinking had some similarities to those of Dewey. But these similarities only go so far. There are many fruitful aspects of classical pragmatism that Rorty tried to cut out from this tradition. These aspects include: action as our starting point, the notion of experience, a modest proposal for truth, and the public as one of the main mechanisms behind politics. I will mention these issues briefly but they will turn up later on in the discussion as well. First, Rortyan pragmatists often begin with issues of knowledge and language, whereas the naturalist way of doing things is to start with action. For example, Rorty (1999, 48) claimed that "we shall never be able to step outside of language." However, one can happily agree as to the importance of language but still argue that experience is not the same thing as its articulation. Lastly, a modest proposal of truth, as it could be called, indicates that no absolute truths are to be found but this does not mean that we should do away with this concept altogether.

Rorty was very keen on emphasizing that Dewey's pragmatism was a precursor to the so-called linguistic turn in philosophy. Many others have argued that classical pragmatists were prone to vote for a more extensive notion of meaning, one that is not restricted to language. This is a perspective in which action sets the scene, so to speak, rather than language, which is actually a very particular form of action. Thus pragmatists have traditionally taken notice of the importance of language for a theory of meaning but they have not claimed that such theory could be reduced to the study of language. For example, Kilpinen (2009, 107) argues that "[a]s a consequence of the linguistic turn, questions of meaning are modeled after the linguistic model, without thinking twice, and what cannot be so modeled is all too quickly deemed as devoid of meaning." What is wrong with such modeling and what things are possibly left out of the picture? As I already indicated, for classical pragmatists questions of meaning arise in relation to action, not only in relation to language, and language-use is a form of action. For some purposes it is probably of use to think of language as a sort of a system that is not controlled by any particular person or institution. However, one can still say that the meaning of words comes down to their use. Even the system-like properties can be explained by the use of language because they have to do with the gradual institutionalization of meanings through habitualization (as discussed later).

As a general philosophical current of thought, pragmatism stresses the practical results of our beliefs. The role that beliefs play is not to mirror the world as such but to resolve problematic actions situations. As Joas (1993, 19) argues, for pragmatists truth "no longer expresses a correct representation of reality in cognition, which can be conceived of using the metaphor of a copy; rather, it expresses an increase of the power to act in relation to an environment." This does not mean that the idea of a copy would be lost, as William James (1975, 102) argues: "To copy a reality is, indeed, one very important way of agreeing with it, but it is far from essential. The essential thing is the process of being guided." To many non-philosophers this issue can seem trivial. However, it has far-reaching implications: we encounter environments in our bodily experience, not just in language. Thus, Rortyan pragmatism is correct in arguing against representationalism as a general model for human meaning making if by representationalism is meant the stance that representations are mirrors of reality.

Surely one can draw maps, for example, but even maps are models, not exact copies. The proof of the pudding is in the eating, as the saying goes, and therefore maps are navigating devices. Copying reality is actually not even possible in the manner that traditional epistemological thought has suggested because our body is involved in our perceptions of the world in a manner that has effects on our perceptions

(Lakoff & Johnson 1999). According to Slingerland (2008, 99): "[t]hought is not language, human beings are not blank slates, and all complex animals – human beings included – inhabit a world permeated by inference-rich, finely textured, and decidedly precultural structures of meaning." For example, the fact that Inuits supposedly have over twenty words for different kinds of snow has often been taken to mean that language very much shapes our world. However, Slingerland (ibid., 112) argues that in fact this example only shows how our *pragmatic interests* in the world shape our language. And what is more, if thought and language are taken to be the same thing it is very hard to explain such everyday phenomena as groping for words in order to express a thought that one has.

Some authors who draw inspiration from Rorty's writings, for example Kivinen and Piiroinen (2006), try to link pragmatism with a view called antirepresentationalism which denies that there is *any* need for the concept of representation. Rorty himself said that "I do not like the metaphor of 'representing the world' or the one that consists of saying that certain propositions can be 'validated' by the world" (Rorty 2007, 37). Rorty's own discussion operates at the level of philosophical epistemology and the real aim of his criticism is the correspondence theory of truth, which says that correct beliefs correspond to reality. For Rortyans it is presumably impossible to discuss the relationships that our concepts have with the world; there are just different ways of describing and redescribing our culture. This argument relies on the presupposition that the evolutionism of pragmatism means a denial of the importance of ontology. The argument presumably also excludes the age-old distinction between the subjective and the objective.

As is well known, ontology deals with what sort of things exist in the world. However, there is no reason to think that ontology always amounts to having a dogmatic ontological stance. That is, if one sticks to a particular ontological view, this does not automatically mean that one thinks of this view as an eternal foundation which is secure and unchanging. Actually, one could argue that even such a view that says that we do not need ontology is an ontological stance because it says something about the nature of reality. Thus, there is really no getting away from the issue of ontology. Pragmatism has traditionally held on to a conception in which the ever-changing nature of reality and of our conceptions is admitted and embraced wholeheartedly. Thus, pragmatism can be said to have an ontological view of reality but it is not one of dogmatic belief: the world can always undergo changes and therefore our views are fallible and cannot rest on solid foundations. This argument is contrary to many isms but it can be labeled with an ism nevertheless: fallibilism. As Westbrook (2005, 4) explains: "the alternative to foundationalism is not skepticism but fallibilism – the conviction that belief, though never certain, is not therefore necessarily dubious. Fallibilism says we may rest content with less than certain yet confident belief. It allows us to affirm our settled convictions, as long as we do so provisionally."

Some authors also link pragmatism with so-called process ontology. Nicholas Rescher (2008),[8] who has famously propagated this linkage, states that "natural existence consists in and is best understood in terms of *process* rather than *things* – of modes of change rather than fixed stabilities." This conception argues that "what a thing *is* consist in what it *does*." Everything in both the natural and the social world (these two are naturally partly overlapping) is ever changing. This might sound very poetic to some ears but it has some concrete implications as well. Most importantly, action – what a "thing" does – is the proper unit of analysis (that is, what a thing does, is the defining feature of that thing). And action is *also* a process. Thus, the focus on action is a natural result of the process view. Kilpinen (2009, 170) has argued that "action comes ahead of knowing, in the sense that the subject first has to establish a steady relationship to his or her world, before closer investigations about it and the truthful statements that they possibly yield come onto the agenda." Naturally it is often difficult to say where a particular action begins and ends. Here it suffices to say that the pragmatist emphasis on habits comes naturally in such a processual view since habits point to the recurrent and continuous features of action. Instead of an exclusive focus on individual actions, pragmatism thus highlights the processes that we call habits. One can also "single out individual deeds, if need be, but the process form is human action's natural form and that is what the habit-term highlights" (Kilpinen forthcoming, 5).

A worry is sometimes voiced that so-called mind first explanations plague the social sciences if we accept realism in any of its forms. The expression "mind-first explanations" was originally coined by Daniel Dennett (1995). His argument was that traditional philosophy has taken for granted that something intelligent – a mind – cannot be a result of non-intelligent processes; there has to be a mind first. Darwin's theory was so revolutionary because it showed that when we take natural selection into account, the mind is precisely explained by such processes. Kilpinen (2000) was probably the first to use this terminology in the context of social theory. According to Kilpinen, pragmatism presents us with an alternative to mind-first explanations as they are used in action theory. Here, these theories presuppose that the mind – reflection – always precedes action. Pragmatists argue that this picture is false because one cannot step outside the flow of action. The radical conclusion sometimes drawn from this is that we cannot make the traditional distinction between the subject and the object because the ever-flowing nature of action means that we are always enmeshed in our environments. This, again, presumably also means that we cannot talk about representations anymore. Rorty's main thesis is, according to Savidan (2007, x-xi), that "the realism-antirealism debate is passé because we are progressing toward a concep-

---

8 This reference is to an article that is published online and therefore there are no references to page numbers.

tion of thought and language that accepts that these may be considered as not containing representations of reality. As realism subsides, it will be possible to escape from the Cartesian problematic of the subject and the object and to break free of the ancient one of appearance and reality."

Some authors working in the field of cognitive science also argue that the distinction into the subjective and the objective belongs to the past. However, whereas the argument of Rortyans runs on the level of epistemology – one cannot really know the difference between appearance and reality – the argument of these cognitive scientists, including some authors with pragmatist influences like Johnson (2007), says that our habits testify to the enmeshing of ourselves and our environments. For example, Määttänen (2009) claims that instead of thinking of dichotomizing the "inner" and "outer" we should enquire into the ways in which the actor and its environment inter- or transact. I think that we should indeed avoid making the subjective and the objective an absolute dichotomy. Once it is realized that these aspects of our experience normally blend in without difficulties, we can rid our theoretical discussions of fruitless debates into how we can really know anything about the world or how we can connect with other human beings. However, there is no reason to throw the baby out with the bathwater. We can and we often should make a distinction between the subjective and the objective or the inner and the outer – for *analytical* purposes. Thus, I am not saying that these issues are metaphysical distinctions or absolute dichotomies but distinctions that are often useful for practical purposes. In some situations, when our habits meet with obstacles for some reason, the divide between the subjective and the objective can feel very real. A denial of this fact easily amounts to classical behaviorism and to its many problems.[9]

In addition, I would argue that there are strictly speaking no purely *inner* representations but still, for analytical purposes, there is no problem in using this concept. We do not have to "ontologize" this concept but it would not be wise to get rid of it altogether. Thus, some sort of an inner environment is necessary if we are to conceptualize the very human phenomenon of premeditation, that is, preselecting among possible lines of conduct. Westbrook (2007, 5) summarizes the pragmatist position on representationalism: "A belief is warranted not if it mirrors the world but if it serves to resolve what Dewey termed the doubtful 'problematic situations' in human experience." The whole background for our beliefs – for the fact that we formulate beliefs – is in responding to problems faced in acting in the world. However, this does not necessarily mean that we do not formulate *representations* at all, as Rortyans often claim. We certainly do so but the context for our representations is in action. Thus, only parts of our environments get represented at any one time – those parts that hap-

---

9 These problems of behaviorism include a mechanical view of action because there is no room for (inner) interpretation.

pen to have relevance for our action processes. Rorty (1999, xxii) said that he hopes "to replace the reality- appearance distinction with the distinction between the more useful and less useful." However, the distinction between the reality and appearance can be very useful in many cases. It is definitely needed if one wants to retain the conceptual possibility of learning from one's mistakes. This possibility has traditionally been labeled as fallibilism.

As has been noted, discussions into whether the concept of representation is warranted or not easily slip into an either or debate. In addition, there is a tendency to view (social) representations as always more or less arbitrary. Some light can be shed onto these questions if one looks more closely at the concept of representation. As a category, it is very broad: it refers to an informational presentation of something. However, obviously there are different kinds of representations – or different aspects of representations. One of the best known discussions of this concept argues that there are three aspects that we should take into account: iconic, indexical and symbolic aspects. This categorization was first introduced by none other than Peirce in a discussion of the properties of signs, but one can use the concept of representation here as well (see Peirce 1998; see also Deacon 1997). Iconic representations are based on resemblance or likeness. Photographs are one instance that readily springs to mind. However, Peirce (1998, 6) argues that the resemblance of photographs "is due to the photographs having been produced under such circumstances that they were physically forced to correspond point by point to nature." Thus, photographs are actually indexical representations which have to do with causal connections or combinations. The mercury in a thermometer is also an example of indexical representation because the way in which it represents temperature is based on causal mechanisms (the expanding of mercury with the rise of temperature). Symbolic representations, or symbols, are those representations that are most familiar to many social scientists: they are more or less arbitrary since they are based on conventional use, that is, on habitual interpretations. To use a familiar example, for some people the US flag symbolizes freedom (among other things), although there is nothing in the stars and stripes as such that would necessitate such an interpretation.

There are (at least) three things that we can learn from this discussion. First, arbitrary symbols are only one aspect of representations. Both Peirce and Deacon argue that even symbols are always based on iconic and indexical relations. Thus, what we have here is not a taxonomy of different signs or representations but a discussion of their different aspects (see also Kilpinen 2008, 222 n5). Even conventional usage (the symbolic aspect) relies on resemblance and on very concrete causal relations and these are *not* purely arbitrary issues. *Usage* implies a material reality that is partly independent of our aspirations. Therefore iconic, indexical and symbolic aspects of representations are usually interrelated. In addition, arguing that the concept of representation is useless because we do not copy reality does not touch upon all the aspects of representations. Furthermore, there *are* some representations that can be characterized as copies of (some aspects of) reality. Very "realistic" photographs are a case in point, although it can easily happen that we almost automatically start to interpret the possible symbolic aspects that iconic representations contain (e.g., if we think of a photograph as containing artistic value). The most common form of representations in social sciences has to do with language – which is where I next direct my attention.

Language, Meaning and Evolution

It is a truism to say that one has to use language if one wants to communicate thoughts to others. However, meanings are not necessarily linguistic even if we would mainly communicate them through language.[10] As mentioned, representations stand for something else; they represent something in a manner that is not identical with that something. In other words, representations *mean* something. For example, for a fox the smell of a rabbit is a representation (or a sign) of the rabbit that has left the smell in its wake.[11] Foxes do not use language but one can argue that the many things mean something to them and therefore their world is not a meaningless collection of purely mechanical reactions. This sort of a semiotic perspective is sometimes called *general semiotics* in contrast to structuralist semiotics, which restricts itself to modeling meanings from the perspective of language (see, e.g., Kilpinen 2008).

Meanings are thus present when one does not react immediately to an environmental stimulus but treats it as a sign of something else. This stimulus can be "internal" as well if it originates in our own inferences. One can say that "a brute stimulus becomes a sign function when an organism considers that stimulus *in connection with* new and future possibilities" (Hildebrand 2008, 50). Such a consideration is a prerequisite for rationality as an operation of self-correction. Knowing is not the same thing as signs, but rather it is "the ability to use signs as evidence for something (past or present), and then adjusting (…) responses informed by these inferences" (ibid., 51). Social constructionism runs the risk of treating knowledge as a purely arbitrary list of things that have been socially learned. Certainly we do have – or we make – lists of things but what easily gets lost in such a conception is the relationship of knowledge to action. "Concepts and ideas are tools or instruments," Hildebrand (ibid., 52) argues. This applies to socially transmitted representations as well: they are there for and in action. Or, in other words, one can say that "[k]nowledge is a strategic assessment of what action-possibilities an object affords" (Lyng & Franks 2002, 62).

10 This also leaves out all the non-linguistic media that we employ in our face-to-face encounters. This is an issue that cannot be discussed here.
11 My thanks to Erkki Kilpinen for suggesting this example (in linguistic and non-linguistic communication).

One foot of classical pragmatism is in the Darwinian revolution, which dramatically affected the mindset of American intellectuals at the end of the nineteenth and the beginning of the twentieth century. The name of Darwin is an ugly word for many sociologists because it has been associated with so-called nativist evolutionary psychology. Nativism in evolutionary psychology is the view that modern social sciences are sadly based on a denial of the idea of human nature and therefore they need to be replaced with a reductive agenda, which postulates universal, innate psychological functions that are presumably based on evolutionary adaptations. The general idea that pragmatists got from Darwin differs from such evolutionary psychology. If we look at evolutionary history, it is obvious that action has been a feature of life forms ever since time began. What is lacking in earlier life forms is the presence of what we call a mind. However, its presence does not mean that action would become embodied. Clark (1999, 350) argues that in human cognition there seems to be "a mixture of highly 'embodied, embedded' strategies and apparently much more abstract and potentially de-coupled strategies, with the creation and manipulation of external symbolic items often functioning as a kind of bridge between the two." To get a glimpse of what this might mean, I will briefly discuss the evolutionary history of our minds (or, our cognition) with the help of Sterelny's (2003) instructive account. This account illuminates the pragmatist idea of the interplay between reflexive and habitual phases of action.

According to Sterelny (2003, 11), "behavioral flexibility is needed in complex environments, for in such environments invariant rules have mediocre rewards." This means that evolutionary reasons can push for behavioral flexibility if the environment of action is such that it is ever-changing. There is evidence that the evolutionary environment of humans is precisely characterized by a push for more flexibility. The major reason for this push has been the "hostility" of the environment.[12] In a hostile environment one can, for example, get eaten by a predator. Sterelny (2003, 26) puts it nicely when he says that "[h]ostile agents *pollute* an animal's informational world by concealment and disguise." In such an environment, the so-called robust tracking of the environment – "the ability to use several [environmental] cues either built-in or learned" (ibid., 28) – is a great advantage over agents that do not share this ability. Sterelny (2003, 29) argues that "[i]ntentional agents have *decoupled representations*. That is to say, we have internal states that track aspects of our world, but which do not have the function of controlling particular behaviors." Human beliefs are an example of such representations. This means that beliefs are not really usually tied to particular behaviors (although they are naturally related to behavior in general). Thus, they make us sensitive to many sources of information because they are not usually tied to very specific environmental cues. Other animals besides humans are also able to rep-

---

12 This is why Sterelny's (2003) book is called *Thought in a Hostile World*.

resent their environments (excluding very simple creatures such as bacteria) but the human specialty is the decoupling of representations from their immediate contexts. In essence, this comes down to increased response-breadth in relation to the environment of action.

Thus, decoupled representations are characterized by increased response-breadth – but they still have to do with responses to our environments. This general evolutionary trend allows for the imaginative play of responses, which is an essential element of human culture. However, what may seem like pure imaginative play may have historical roots in very concrete action situations. One can therefore argue, alongside classical pragmatists, that the meaning of representations comes down to their effect on our behavior. For example, a representation of a dog activates different images and the point of these images is the way in which they prepare us for acting with dogs (e.g., stroking them or taking them for a walk). Naturally things become more complicated with more complex and abstract representations. If one thinks of "society" it is not so clear what the reference of this concept is. However, one could still say that even the meaning of abstract concepts has to do with attitudes towards some referential object(s). In this case these attitudes are not that specific but, rather, more generalized. This is an issue to which I will return when I discuss Mead's ideas.

Evolution has to do with increased success in staying alive and reproducing. It is easy to see why a "mind" would be very helpful in this regard: it enables one to evaluate different hypotheses when one encounters problematic action situations. This enablement is made possible by the increase in response-breadth that Sterelny discusses. One can use the concept of hypotheses although we are naturally not discussing scientific hypotheses here – but hypotheses they are nevertheless, that is, ways of evaluating different lines of conduct *before actually responding*. Dennett (1996, ch. 4) has argued that humans are "Popperian creatures" because we are capable of "preselection among all the possible behaviors or actions, so that the truly stupid moves are weeded out before they're hazarded in 'real life.'" Thus, Popperian creatures have an inner environment that can perform such maneuvers of preselection. Naturally, pragmatists do not argue that our action would exclusively be about conscious trying out of hypotheses. For the most part, action is habitual but there is still a place for conscious, reflexive thought. Mind-first explanations tend to make a special case into the norm: they (e.g., rational choice theory) claim that reflexive pondering would be our main or even our only form of action, whereas it is more like an exception in the normal flow of habitual action.

It is possible to argue that strictly speaking the mind cannot be located within our heads. For example, Mead presumed that we can locate the mind in the relationship between action and its environment. Our action is so enmeshed in our environments that it is possible to speak of a process of *trans*action. Dewey and Bentley (1949, 132-133) contrasted the concept of transaction with both interaction and self-action:[13] in self-action "things are viewed as acting under their own powers" (they act on their own) whereas in interaction a "thing is balanced against thing in causal interconnection" (they exist independently of the interaction). Transaction differs from both of these modes because it attributes no elements or entities that would exist independently of the process that they are a part of. Modern cognitive scientists would say that our cognition is distributed and thus not restricted inside one's head (see Hutchins 2006).

The idea that we mainly adopt a reflexive attitude in times of action crises can sound too instrumental to many ears. What about daydreaming and fantasy, do not these things exist? Well, they certainly do exist. For example, Veblen used the concept of idle curiosity to refer to our natural tendency to be interested in what happens around us, without necessarily having any instrumental aims. One can agree that "curiosity – epistemic hunger – must drive any powerful learning system" (Dennett 1996, 121). However, pure fantasy will not get us very far without a critical input given by a reflexive attitude that picks out the most appropriate associations from the flow of associations. What is appropriate depends, of course, very much on the given situation. And, as I already have said, the situation does not have to be the concrete situation that we happen to be in because many of our representations are "decoupled" from the immediate contexts of action. In addition, one can make the claim that some crises are chronic and their chronic nature offers an explanation for many specialist occupations. For example, health problems are endemic and that is why we have physicians (Shilling 2008, 32).

Pragmatism and Science

Sometimes sociologists, especially sociologists of science, are very critical of the possibilities of science. At least it often appears that they have a critical stance because they tend to reduce the findings and evidence used by science to its social context. Of course, no sociologist in his right mind would be willing to argue that the social context plays no role also in science. Science is, after all, an institution and it shares many features with other institutions. For example, the day-to-day operations of scientists can be as habitual as the operations in other institutions. However, science is clearly different in some respects because its constituting habits are more reflexive than in many other institutions. Rorty (1999, xxi) argued that "Dewey (…) talked a lot about bringing 'scientific method' into philosophy, but he never was able to explain what this method was." I disagree with Rorty – although there might not be a particular method to science. The following elaborates on some Deweyan ideas.

---

13   Dewey and Bentley write all of these concepts with a hyphen (inter-action etc.). For the sake of clarity, I have abandoned this style of writing.

Introduction: Grounds for Pragmatism

Science does not produce absolute truths but, rather, theories that are in connection with particular research questions (see, e.g., Haack 2007 or Kivinen and Piiroinen 2006). Theories do not aim at explaining all of reality at once (whatever such an all-encompassing explanation might even mean). It is one thing to do science and another to treat science as an *ism*. There are two things wrong with this scient*ist* attitude. First, it makes sense to enquire into anything within frameworks that are more or less clearly defined. Thus, there is first a problem and then we need to probe into its possible answers. It is mere "paper doubt" (Peirce's phrase) to doubt all of our beliefs at once (in any area of life); in practice, it is neither possible nor desirable (Bertilsson 2009). Second, we can always encounter new problems that shake the foundations of our habits, which means that there is no point in searching for supposedly permanent solutions for any problems that we might have.

However, such arguments that claim science to be nothing but a social construction simply fail to see the role that evidence plays in inquiry in general, and especially in scientific inquiry. Following Misak (2000, 77), it can be argued that it makes sense to talk of beliefs only if there are reasons that can speak for or against them. A belief is by definition about something. As a pragmatist, Misak connects these reasons for or against a belief with the consequences of beliefs. Thus we can say that modern scientists are in the business of looking at the consequences of beliefs through experiential inquiry – that is, through evidence gathered by conducting experiments. It is certainly the case that our theories have effects on what we see – it is data, after all, not random perceptions – but it is an exaggeration to claim that theories would determine our empirical findings. If this exaggeration were true there would be no need to conduct any empirical inquiry in the first place! Of course, individual scientists can close their eyes to the evidence at hand but this is precisely where the social character of science can be of help. In science, beliefs are "checked" with the help of many social mechanisms (peer reviewing, active social competition etc.). Social checking of beliefs can in some cases lead to the strengthening of stereotypes but, in principle, individual beliefs are more untrustworthy. Sociologists also often make a big fuss of the almost trivial fact that we always have a perspective on something (whatever that something happens to be). From this undeniable fact the conclusion is sometimes drawn that perspectives can never be reconciled. Naturally, reconciling perspectives is no easy feat but Misak, as well as Sen (2010), argue that it is possible to try to take many perspectives into account. I would add that this is what makes social beliefs more accurate (in general): they are based on many perspectives.

Modern science is research science, as Mead (1936) argued, not a list of eternal truths. Even theories are not summaries of truths but rather theories are a way of relating to reality and transacting with it. Even though many theories can seem very abstract, their final meaning – or their final interpretant (to use a Peircean expression) – comes down to their effects on the relationship between the actor and its (or his or her) environment. Classical pragmatists were among the first to notice that this scientific attitude has implications for philosophy as well because it is the opposite of traditional philosophical views that were concentrated with postulating transhistorical truths. Science proceeds as human thinking does in general: through problematic situations. The "normal" phase of action, in science and in general, is one in which habits reign. This much was indicated by Thomas Kuhn's famous discussion of the paradigms of science. These habits, however, often meet with obstacles due to changing environments and circumstances; for example, we find novel data that do not fit with the initial explanation. Such obstacles are not something to avoid whatever the cost (which is often the attitude in other spheres of life). Rather, it is often fruitful to *generate* problems.

Haack has vehemently opposed both cynical views that tend to discredit science and those conceptions of science that see it as progressing according to an inevitable logic of its own. She characterizes her own position with a term originally coined by Peirce: it is one of "critical common-sensism." This is a position that "acknowledges, like the New Cynicism [authors critical of science], that observation and theory are inter-dependent, that scientific vocabulary shifts and changes meaning, and that science is a deeply social enterprise" (Haack 2007, 23). Science is not that different from everyday reasoning and other forms of inquiry (journalism, for example) – if and when these other forms also rely on a mix of experiential evidence and reasoning. Haack also argues that there really is nothing like a scientific method as such. However, what does set science apart is "the vast range of 'helps' to inquiry devised by generations of scientists to overcome natural human limitations" (ibid., 25). These helps include not only instruments of observation but also models and metaphors and techniques related to statistical reasoning. Thus, science is an extension of common sense but a critical one at that; it is more systematic and self-controlled in its operations. Thus, one does not have to be a cynic to agree on the fallibility of science: as it is a way of correcting our habits, it *cannot* but be fallible.

The Concept of Habit

The concept of habit is not uncommon in popular discussions. For example, in his book *Outliers. The Story of Success* (2008), Malcolm Gladwell argues that industrious practice (at the minimum, 10,000 hours!) is the major reason for success in any area of life. Naturally the parents one happens to have and the larger cultural context do play a role, but the best thing that these factors can give us is opportunities for meaningful practice. Gladwell does not use the concept of habit but in a previous book of his the theme related to the issue of how "we toggle back and forth between our conscious and unconscious modes of thinking, depending on the situation" (Gladwell

2005, 12). The ability to make decisions without consciously thinking about the issue at hand is an ability that, according to Gladwell, develops through constant practice.

It should come as no surprise that popular discussions have tapped into the importance of unconscious thought since it is a theme that also runs through modern cognitive science. The working of the unconscious has been a recurrent theme in psychology, especially since Freud. Recent psychology often taps into the foundation role of sensomotoric proclivities in cognition in a manner that is quite alien to Freudian psychology (see Claxton 2005). The phenomenon of habituality is therefore actively researched by current psychology. For example, Bargh and Chartrand (1999, 462), who review research done on the subject, argue that "most of a person's everyday life is determined not by their conscious intentions and deliberate choices but by mental processes that are put into motion by features of the environment and that operate outside of conscious awareness and guidance." According to them, the good thing about such habitual processes – or nonconscious processes, as they call them – is that they are "effortless, very fast, and many of them can operate at any given time" (ibid., 476). A more recent discussion by Noë (2009, 98) suggests that even "[j]udgement, deliberation, [and] decision making take place in a context" and therefore even these "higher" functions are not habit-free. Surprisingly few of the discussions on nonconscious cognition in psychology and cognitive science explicitly refer to pragmatism. There are, however, notable exceptions (e.g., Slingerland 2008; Johnson 2006). Of course, this neglect goes both ways because not that many discussions in the pragmatist camp take notice of the similar themes approached in the behavioral sciences (as cognitive science, psychology and the like are often collectively called).

The concept of habit is without doubt of central importance for pragmatism. However, traditional philosophical expositions sometimes tend to downplay this central concept because their interest often tends to focus on epistemological issues. Nevertheless, the concept of habit cannot be avoided since the main relevance of pragmatism is in the realm of action theory. It is common to think of simple routines in the context of habits. Then the basic idea is that we are usually conscious of our actions but when certain actions get repeated often enough, they tend to habitualize and become mere routines. This idea is to be found, for example, in the social constructionism of Peter Berger and Thomas Luckmann ([1966] 1995). Thus the basic model is that we consciously act, but eventually our action "sinks" below consciousness. This sort of argument often tends to identify consciousness, language and knowledge together.

The routine-like character of action is undoubtedly one of the meanings of the term "habit." For example, opening a door is usually a routine in the sense that one does not have to think the operation through. Habits can often also be very restrictive in the sense that they tend to direct action into pre-existing channels. As Shilling (2008, 15) argues, "while individuals die, habits can live on in objects and technologies, and also in customs and traditions." Furthermore: "habits can function as massively important conserving agents which not only economize and simplify our actions, but which have the potential to reproduce social structures" (ibid.). Thus, habitualized action is such that one does not have to concentrate on it consciously and thus this conscious pondering can be left for other activities – or for fine-tuning whatever one is doing at the moment.

One of the most thorough reviews of the uses of the habit concept in sociology has been presented by Camic (1986). According to his analysis, one can distinguish a habit continuum. On the lower levels of this continuum, one finds dispositions to perform elementary and specific activities, whereas on the upper reaches habit refers to the broader conduct of life or to the idea of character (ibid., 1045-1046). Even though Camic (1988, 958) has argued that Meadian uses of the term lie on the lower levels, I think it is clear that pragmatists also think of habits in the broader sense. In this broader sense, "[c]omplex chains of activity may be based on organized sets of habits" (Baldwin 1988, 955). Thus, in Meadian parlance, the social attitudes of the environment and our associations and responses towards those environments can be integrated in a generalized other. However, such integrated unity is not matter-of-course but rather something to strive for.

Classical sociologists like Durkheim and Weber had a place for the concept of habit in their theoretical schemes – even though they were somewhat ambiguous about its relevance – but eventually the concept "was written out of the history of modern social theory" (Camic 1986, 1074) by Talcott Parsons. Camic argues that the main reason for the loss of "habit" from the tool-kit of sociology has to do with an aversion to behaviorism. There certainly are some affinities with behaviorism and pragmatism. Both take seriously the fact that there are different stimuli in our environments. However, these thought currents are not the same thing. For pragmatists, stimuli relate to what we happen to be doing. For example, perceptions are very selective in the sense that we often pick out those features of the environment that we expect to find. Therefore the relationship between stimuli and reactions is not mechanical. In the words of Cook (2006, 70), the "stimulus and response reciprocally affect one another."

Habits are, in a sense, adaptations – in relation to the environment in which they have been formed. This does not mean that they would by definition be functional in relation to some *social system*, for example (as in Parsons' thought). As Shilling (2008, 13) argues, habits are self-perpetuating once they have been constituted. For example, habits affect our perceptual awareness by selecting familiar stimuli from all the rest and this is why they can be immune to stimuli that contradict their nature. In general, the point of adaptations is that "they form connections, or linkages, between organisms and the world they inhabit" (Plotkin 2003, 29). The role of adaptations in evolutionary theory is to explain how some consequences of genetic mutations can lead to advantageous changes in organisms: some mutations fit particular environments of action better than others and these functional mutations are called adaptations. However, things are not as straightforward as might seem. There are both cases where a trait that originally has no function acquires a function and cases where one function co-opts some other function than the one that it originally had. Thus, non-functional traits can either become adaptations or they can become adapted to a different "purpose" than originally was the case (the technical term for the latter phenomenon is *exaptation*). Furthermore, "the existence of multiple adaptations places structural and energetic constraints on all of them" (ibid., 33).

Habits are the result of learning processes, not the result of changes in our genetic make-up. However, Plotkin's discussion of the complexity of adaptations has some bearing on the issue of habits as well. One can thinks of cases where some habit that has developed in a particular environment eventually extends into another environment. For example, when one visits another country one usually encounters familiar cues that are often not quite what they seem. Thus, our habits can map onto environmental cues also in cases where these cues are not exactly the same as the original ones. Even more interesting are those cases, to use the same quote from Plotkin (2003, 33), where "the existence of multiple adaptations places structural and energetic constraints on all of them." In such a case, habits are not fully integrated with each other. Quite often it can feel like habits pull us in different directions (the structural constraint). There is also a limit as to how complicated and how many habits one can learn (the energetic constraint).

Habits can be thought of as *phases* of action rather than its determinants. Saying that what one did on some occasion was more or less habitual can naturally act as an explanation of sorts. However, there are some real issues involved in seeing habituality as a phase of action. First, it indicates the processual nature of action – that is, action is a process in which habits and deliberations take turns. Second, and related to the former, is the basic idea behind pragmatism that humans – and other animals, one might add – are always active. Thus, there are no passive states of inactivity but rather different kinds of action; some of these kinds can, of course, be more active than others. The consequence of this tenet is, as Shilling (2008, 12) illuminatively explains, that "[i]t is not the initiation of action that has to be explained, but the characteristics of how people act in particular situations." He also argues that action consists of phases and the main phases of action are *habit, crisis* and *creativity*. However, what Schilling tends not to see is that it is useful to see these phases as often overlapping. This means that things are not either/or; for example, the habit phase is not either on or off. Even the creative phase of action utilizes our habits. For instance, learning a skill – such as driving a car – usually means that its mastery becomes habitual in the sense that we do not have to ponder upon its rudimentary aspects. However, we do not become totally non-creative towards this skill once it becomes habitual. Rather, well developed habituality enables creativity because instead of concentrating on the elementary aspects, one can concentrate on fine-tuning and developing the skill in question. This is why one can call the pragmatist conception of habits reflexive habituality, rather than, for example, routine habituality (Kilpinen 2000).

One thing that should be discussed in relation to habits is the way in which they are related to individuals. For example, Turner (1994) has claimed that many practice theories are not capable of explaining how practices are shared. This same critique can be made in relation to theories of habits. However, according to Kilpinen (2009a, 113), this problem only arises if we view practices as some sort of baggage or possessions to carry around: "Turner's idea about tradition-*cum*-habit being something that an individual carries with oneself and then transmits – like a father gives an inherited gold watch to his son – is not necessarily a defining characteristic of traditions." Kilpinen argues that rather than viewing practices and habits according to a logic of possessive individualism (as our possessions) we are better off if we follow a so-called participatory notion. Habits need not be exactly the same for everyone involved but a "'working agreement' about basics is all that is needed" (ibid.). Such a participatory view – habits are shared in the sense that they allow for *participation* in common activities – has the advantage that it leaves room for individual interpretation because it does not make the unconvincing claim that cultures are monolithic.

Gross (2009) has analyzed social mechanisms with the help of pragmatist notions of habits. His way of using pragmatism is illuminating because it brings forth fundamental issues having to do with the notion of habituality. Gross proposes that social mechanisms (the causes in social explanations) "are best thought of as chains or aggregations of problem situations and the effects that ensue as a result of the habits actors use to resolve them" (ibid., 375). As mentioned, pragmatists usually make the claim that problematic action situations are such crises that they tend to lead to novel responses. Thus, first there is a habit and then there is a crisis and, its corollary, doubt, due to the environmental changes. Sooner or later this situation is followed by the elimination of doubt with the help of a novel habit. What Gross adds to this picture is the argument that even in problem situations people tend to rely on habitual responses and not on novel solutions. Naturally there are unique historical chains of events in which such novelty is present. Thus Gross admits that novel ways of responding are always a possibility – but not all situations are prone to encourage the formation of new habits.

A Note on Pragmatist Literature

The classical canon of pragmatism naturally has other names besides those of G. H. Mead and John Dewey. For example, Charles Cooley discussed the social nature of the self in quite similar terms as Mead did (see, e.g., Cooley 1956). Furthermore, William I. Thomas can be credited as a pragmatist in sociology and Arthur Bentley in political science. However, I have decided to concentrate on using the work of Dewey and Mead. One of the reasons for this solution is the simple fact that one has to draw a line somewhere. It could also be argued that of all the canonical names of classical pragmatism Mead and Dewey are the ones that have most relevance for social theory, especially in relation to the theme of action and social structures. There are problems in reading both Mead and Dewey, although these problems differ in kind. With Mead's work, there are difficulties due to the fact that many of his published books are based on notes and on unpublished manuscripts. In the case of Dewey, the problems are quite different in character: they have to do with his massive output because Dewey's collected works consist of 37 volumes. I am not intending to do an exegetical study of either of these authors. This means that I am not tracing the development of Mead's thought, for example, or the way in which Dewey changed his mind on some matters. Fortunately, there already are very illuminating studies published that deal with these issues (on Mead, see Joas 1985; Cook 1993; on Dewey, see Westbrook 1991). What I *have* done is to look at what Mead and Dewey have to say about action, social structures and the role that habits and reflectivity play in all this.

Of contemporary authors, I have concentrated on those that can be said to elaborate the social theoretical ideas of the figures mentioned above. In this regard, the most important contemporary inspirers of my work are Hans Joas and Erkki Kilpinen. It is probably no exaggeration to say that Joas' book *The Creativity of Action* (1996, published in German in 1992) was one of the main reasons why pragmatism was brought into many discussions on social theory in the 1990s. Of course, it was not only due to this book that pragmatism gained new momentum; for example, Joas' earlier work had paved the way (Joas 1993; 1985). And naturally there are other, just as important, names that have kept the pragmatist heritage alive in social theory. The role of Richard Rorty has already been dealt with but the name of Richard Bernstein should also be mentioned. Bernstein has, for example, discussed the connection between pragmatism and hermeneutics (see Bernstein 1983). However, since it is not so much social philosophy that I am dealing with, those contemporary authors who elaborate on pragmatist action and social theory have been the centers of my attention. For example, the contribution made by Geoffrey Hodgson is one that I have found useful.

Mead and Intersubjectivity

Chapter 2 has the title *The Over- or the Undersocialized Conception of Man? Practice Theory and the Problem of Intersubjectivity*. Practice theory has gained momentum in recent years and it has many commonalities with pragmatism: both highlight the situated and corporeal character of human activity. Thus, for both theory traditions, it is the practical nature of our involvement with the world that is of interest. It could be argued that pragmatism and practice theory are cousins – or even brothers in arms. As can be seen from their respective names, both theoretical traditions highlight the importance of the practical realm. Kilpinen (2009, 107) has argued that one of the aims of practice theory is to "reconsider and perhaps undo some of those conclusions that have been drawn as consequences of the linguistic turn." It is certainly a feature of some practice theories – if not most of them – to reconsider linguistic theories of meaning. However, this feature is not shared by all of them. For example, Reckwitz (2002) tries to incorporate the insights of constructionism, which usually underscore linguistic aspects, into practice theory.

There are thus many versions of practice theory but one famous proponent is Margaret Archer who is also known as a spokesperson for so-called critical realism. Archer argues that the pragmatism of G. H. Mead leads to an oversocialized conception of selfhood. Mead's views presumably leave no room for individual agency as it seems to be the society that does the talking (so to speak). The commonalities between pragmatism and practice theory should certainly be taken into account but, contrary to Archer's claims, Mead is not quite the constructionist that Archer tries to make him out to be. Mead does indeed present a socialized view of selfhood but this is a "meta-sociological" argument rather than a substantial sociological claim. In other words, Mead is discussing the general outlines of the process in which our selfhood develops and in which we learn to take the role of the other towards ourselves. Self-consciousness, by definition, is about being able to see oneself as an object. Mead is not saying that *the contents* of our selfhood would always be dictated by our social relations even though we tend to anticipate the possible reactions of others towards our actions. Thus, we can say that intersubjectivity precedes proper, rational subjectivity – and not the other way around. This is why humans are socially oriented even when acting alone: we tend to take the attitudes of non-present others towards our conceived actions. Naturally the intensity with which the attitudes of others are felt is different when others are actually present. However, we can always imagine and remember the attitudes of others even when we are not interacting with them. This chapter also outlines the general idea of how habitual action produces social structures. The latter do not "colonize" action since there is a place for individual agency or internal conversations (in Archer's terminology); this place is especially, although not necessarily exclusively, situated in those phases of action where action meets with obstacles due to changes in the (social) environment. Mead visions a continuous dialogue between the "I" and the "me;" that is, between our spontaneous reactions and societal habits. However, this dialogue is probably more frantic in those problematic situations.

Next I will discuss some topics that give a broader picture of Mead's views. I will also say something about the possible criticisms that can be directed at Mead – and at my arguments.

Mead in Context

A few years ago, Gillespie (2005, 19) asked the following question: "How many different George Herbert Mead's have the there been?" At first sight this question might sound absurd; surely there has been only one G. H. Mead. However, Gillespie was drawing our attention to the fact that there have been quite a few different Mead interpretations. Indeed, so many interpretations that "[f]ew theorists have, posthumously, been as productive as Mead" (ibid.). As in the case of many classical authors, there is a danger of a presentist reading when one deals with Mead's writings. This type of reading refers to interpreting his work purely from the perspective of our present interests. These interests are certainly a legitimate starting point but one should be careful not to let them blind us to the original context of Mead's thought (or to any author's context for that matter). Da Silva (2006) has distinguished between three different influential sociological readings of his work: those of Herbert Blumer, Jürgen Habermas and Hans Joas. As is well known, Blumer was the first proponent of so-called symbolic interactionism. His interpretation "tends to subsume, against the spirit of Mead, the category of human action to that of symbolic interaction" (ibid., 26). Blumer's way of reading Mead is thus in conflict with the starting point of pragmatism, which is action, and is thus not the reading that I advocate. Habermas, for his part, is somewhat too keen on developing a "linguistically minded sociological theory" (ibid., 31). Therefore, if one follows da Silva's conceptualization, my reading falls within the Joasian camp. Da Silva argues that Joas fails to enlighten his readers on the way in which Mead's thoughts developed throughout his career. This critique does not seem justified (see Joas 1985). However, I do not really have to take a stance on this issue since I am not conducting a Meadian exegesis.

Mead's thought has sometimes elicited the labels of behaviorism and social behaviorism. The latter is a concept coined by Charles Morris, the editor of Mead's lectures published as *Mind, Self and Society*. Cook (2006, 72) has argued that:

> Both terms are unfortunate in that they conceal the functionalist roots of Mead's social psychology while suggesting an affinity between Mead's ideas and those of classical behaviorism. (…) Mead's aim was never to restrict the subject matter of

psychology to publicly observable behavior in the manner of classical behaviorism: he always intended to keep the study of the mental as a legitimate and central part of psychology, but he wanted to approach the mental functionally, as a dimension of conduct.

Behaviorists argue that it is impossible to get inside people's heads and therefore science should restrict itself to studying observable behavior. This attitude can be justified if it is used as a reaction against the introspective methodologies of traditional philosophers. Traditional philosophers – as well as many contemporary ones – have studied their own consciousness by non-systematic introspection and often tended to reveal more or less idiosyncratic phenomena. They also tend to forget the intrinsic connection of the mental to the material world (they thus see problems where there are none). What does the connecting is, unsurprisingly, action. Like behaviorists, Mead would therefore be the first to argue that action should be on the agenda of a naturalist philosophy of mind and social science but in his hands this stance does not lead to a denial of mental phenomena. Rather, the argument is that mental phenomena are a dimension of conduct or, as I would formulate it, as a *subclass* of phenomena of action. In this case, functionality refers to the role that consciousness plays in action: it facilitates action by looking at its (possible) obstacles. Thus, we can say that habits have a cognitive function (they economize actions, as discussed earlier) and, in addition, that consciousness has a function in relation to action processes. One could also say that rather than label Mead a (social) behaviorist, it is more apt to call him, in addition to being a pragmatist, a representative of the functional school in psychology.

As mentioned, social constructionists often argue that our environment is socially constructed. Rather than emphasizing the role of active agency in constructing this environment, the argument then is that it is our "culture" that does the constructing for us with the help of different kinds of media (especially texts). Meadian pragmatism gives more priority for active agency as there is always the unpredictable and impulsive role of our mental associations in the role of the "I" (in relation to the social habits of the "me"). However, this does not mean that action would *produce* our environment(s). Of course, in some cases it can do so, at least to some extent (i.e., when we literally produce something) but generally speaking this is not the case. For example, grass serves as nourishment only for those animals that are able to digest it. Cows do not construct the grass but we can say that the action process of a cow, which in this case is related to its eating behavior, singles out grass as a very powerful stimulus. Mead (1936, 140) says the following:

> You may say that the object is there before the animal, but it is not there as food. The animal comes with a stomach that can digest only certain things, and so determines its own world. Its own sensitiveness, its own methods of reaction, its own fashion of dealing with the world make a new world out of it.

Introduction: Grounds for Pragmatism

By being sensitive towards some features of our environments we make a new world out of it, as Mead here says. Grass certainly grows without any help from cows but cows partake in its process of growth and decay. Social constructionism easily leads to a view in which we literally produce – or construct – our environments by the more or less knowledge-based images that we happen to have of them. This view is understandable if one presupposes that we can never tackle reality as such but only our conceptions of reality. And indeed, in many cases there is no need to posit a reality totally independent of our conceptions. Earlier I mentioned Hacking's concept of an interactive kind which refers to the fact that "[w]ays of classifying human beings interact with the human beings who are classified" (Hacking 1999, 31). Our cultural environment – which is enmeshed with material non-cultural reality – very much consists of such kinds. Thus, if someone is labeled a criminal this can change the way that someone views him- or herself (in criminology this view is known as labeling theory). Interactive kinds are different from the objects of natural sciences which Hacking calls natural or indifferent kinds. For example, volcanoes are indifferent to what we happen to think of them and therefore they do not interact with our classifications. However, it is clear that the most interesting cases ("kinds") consist of a mix of both natural and interactive kinds. For example, autism probably has a neurological basis but many autists react positively to autism-sensitive teaching (more on this issue later).

It is important to take note that it is our action-based reactions towards reality that count, not only those having to do with discourse or knowledge. Furthermore, even discourses and knowledge are reactions towards our environments, although they are often very abstract reactions. The objective qualities of objects are out there – independently of our reactions. However, being sensitive to some objects and not others can constitute a wholly different world. In part, this depends on the organs and receptive qualities that we happen to have, that is, on our bodily capabilities. These are not socially constructed or dependent on our social beliefs (or individual beliefs, for that matter). Some authors have gone as far as to claim that our bodily being affects even abstract thought processes. Lakoff and Johnson (1999, 34-35) argue that our bodies shape conceptual structures in many ways. For example, this happens through bodily projections: something is in *front* of something or at the *back* of something. We build abstract metaphors on the basis of these bodily projections (thus, the future is something that *lies ahead*). Furthermore, the learning of culture is essentially about social attitudes towards all kinds of objects (abstract ones included).

Mead's conceptualization of the "I" and the "me" easily lead to confusion. For example, if one thinks of them as clearly distinct parts of selfhood, then one ends up with a more or less schizophrenic picture: we have an "I" that occasionally takes control and sometimes gives way to the "me." Naturally there are psychological cases where this sort of actual role-taking does indeed take place; just think of Alfred Hitchcock's *Psycho* where the main character has literally internalized the social attitudes of his mother. However, these are pathological cases and hardly apply as a general frame for selfhood.

Lyng and Franks (2002, 176-177) argue that "Mead's distinction between the 'I' and the 'me' refers specifically to the dynamic between a contingent body capable of spontaneous, unpredictable behavior and a social mind that gives meaningful form to this behavior." Thus, the contingency and impulsivity of our bodily reactions is what is meant by the "I" whereas the "me" refers to our social habits. This is not to say that the "I" and the "me" would always be opposed to each other, as in Freud's view of culture repressing the bodily (i.e., sexual) aspects of our behavior. Rather, the "I" and the "me" often go hand in hand. For example, an inarticulate intuition that we might have can receive full form through reflecting on existing habits. Or one can also work on one's impulses (the "I") through habitual training (the "me"). It is all too easy – and fashionable – to refer to the interaction between nature and culture (see, for example Ridley 2004). This interaction is not exactly the same thing as the interaction between the "I" and the "me." However, this reference is worth making because it challenges the way in which we easily view something as being either nature or nurture.

This issue can be illustrated with an example dealing with the alleged "nativity" of language (that is, seeing it as a product of nature). Some authors (Noam Chomsky being the most famous example) have argued that without an innate language "instinct" it is impossible to explain how children are able to become fluent speakers because the instances of grammatical rules that they are provided with in their natural environments are so fragmentary. That is, it is very hard to imagine how children can pick up the rules of grammar even though these rules are only implicitly present in their formative years. However, Deacon (1997) argues that it is not helpful to see language as primarily a native capacity but rather to look at the evolution of language. It has been a process in which both the users of language and language(s) have evolved. Thus, our brains have evolved to master language but in the long run only those grammatical rules get transmitted to children which children are able to learn. Analogously to the case of biological evolution, we can therefore think of a selection mechanism that favors those grammatical rules that are easy to learn. What this all means is that there indeed exists a complex interaction between our biological and mental abilities and the cultural rules of language. It is possible to extrapolate from these results by arguing that the "I" and the "me" are factors in such an interaction. Thus, social and cultural habits have their say in human matters but some habits get transmitted more easily than others, due to their interaction with the "I." For example, such habits that are very complex and psychologically demanding (e.g., hard to remember or difficult to execute) will probably not spread very far. Of course, to paraphrase Bourdieu, these kinds of habits can be used in a game of status distinctions but this is another issue.

Archer (2007) has continued her preoccupation with reflexivity since the writing of my chapter dealing with Mead (it was written in 2007). She states that "[h]uman beings are distinctive not as the bearer of projects, which is a characteristic people share with every animal, but because of their reflexive ability to design (and redesign) many of the projects they pursue" (Archer 2007, 7). This citation bears witness to the important role reflexivity has for her; it is a – or actually *the* – distinctive feature of humanity. One should also note her way of using the idea of projects that relates them only to goal-oriented action. This differs from some authors, such as Heiskala (2003), who sees projects as *discursively conscious plans* of action. For Archer (ibid., 9), projects can become habitualized, or as she says, "embodied knowledge." If and when they do so, only "a change of circumstances can make us realise that (…) they are (…) successful social practices which have become taken for granted." One can interpret this by saying that also projects can – and often do – become habitualized. Archer maintains that reflexivity is "prior to, relatively autonomous from and possesses causal efficacy in relation to structural or cultural properties" (ibid., 15). This sort of an underscoring of reflexivity can be justified as an argumentative strategy because there clearly have been theoretical attempts to downplay the role of reflexivity in sociology and social theory. However, I think that she overextends her argument. Reflexivity can be relatively autonomous from structural properties and it possesses causal efficacy in relation to those properties but this does not necessarily mean that reflexivity is *prior to* these factors. Rather, it is born out of a complex interaction with structural properties.

Archer, as said before, is right to point out that for Mead a self can only arise within a social process. However, this is not to say that we are some sort of "social dupes" always acting in accordance with the dictates of others. Of course there can be such other-directed persons as the main character in Woody Allen's movie *Zelig* who can change his identity in an instant from an Orthodox Jew to a Native American according to the social environment he finds himself in. However, it would be bordering on the ridiculous to claim that this was what Mead was after. Mead can be interpreted as arguing that our selfhood is partly constituted in "the stories that we tell ourselves" (Gross 2002, 54). We cannot tell ourselves just any story we happen to like but one which is rooted in our social setting and in our biographical background, that is, in our habits.

In general one can say that the idea of morality is related to the inhibitory nature of cognitive operations. This idea is not derived from Freud, who thought that it is the superego that inhibits and controls our animal urges, which tend to be mainly (if not totally) sexual. The voice of the superego comes from our parents and it represents the repressive elements of civilization. Pragmatists would agree that mental associations are often plentiful and therefore some inhibiting has to be done (in order to introduce some order into the confusion). The inhibition of associations is not due to a supposedly repressive civilization but due to the fact that mental associations are indeed plentiful, and, as a result, *rationality* requires that only those associations get picked up that are relevant for the particular context(s) of action. Rationality inhibits and it is concerned with self-control. Rational reconstruction picks up the relevant stimuli that are coming from the environment and responds to these in a more or less suitable manner. Inhibition can, of course, turn into real repression, but that is not the normal case and so it should not be represented as a model for morality in general. In this argument, morality does not differ so much from other forms of mental inhibiting. It has to do with the good; that is, with the desired results of our conduct.

If Mead does not deny reflexivity its place, is it possible that he exaggerates its importance? Joas implies this in his critique of Mead. He argues that Mead, among others (Dewey and Charles Horton Cooley), developed his "theories of the self as an attempt to replace a substantialist understanding of the soul with a functionalist definition of the psychical [as a phase of action] and an intersubjectivist explanation of the constitution of the self" [selfhood as an objectivation based on the attitude of others'] (Joas 2008, 122-123). The problem with this sort of an understanding is presumably that "it loses sight of another dimension of the older notion of the soul – namely, the sacred character of each human being" (ibid.). The sacred character of human beings, in Joas' argument, is needed if one wants to defend human rights. It is indeed true that the replacement of a notion of a mystical soul by the self as an object of empirical research was on Mead's agenda. It is also true that as a consequence a dogmatic belief in a sacral and eternal soul has to go; Mead was, after all, a committed naturalist who thought that supernatural beliefs have no place in a post-Darwinian science. However, Joas' criticism is not without its problems. First, a belief in a sacred and eternal soul introduces more problems than it solves. For example, where does it come from? Second, and this bears more heavily on the argument, there seems to be no empirical foundation for a belief in an immutable soul. To give Joas due credit, naturally it might happen that one could overdo the self-conscious aspect of our selves and then come to the conclusion that all humans lacking a certain level of self-consciousness are not properly speaking humans. However, this conclusion is easily avoided if one remembers that self-consciousness is, even in the "best" of cases, only a phase of action – in a process where habituality is foundational.

The Case of Autists

It has been suggested that Mead presents a "unifying theory for sociology" (see Baldwin 2002). However, many Meadian themes touch upon meta-sociological issues rather than upon sociology as such. The case of autistic persons is illuminating in this context because autists lack some of the social skills that sociologists usually take for granted. More specifically, I use the case of autistic persons to hit emphasize the point about self-consciousness being dependent on intersubjective sociality. Autists often do not have normal, habitual social relations with others, and this is the reason why they also lack a unified self or self-consciousness – they are unable to see themselves through the eyes of others, as parts in a web of social relations. It is often argued that autists lack a proper "theory of mind" (Baron-Cohen 1995). This means that they do not necessarily postulate intentions and other mental phenomena for other people and their actions. Identifying intentions involves a theoretical postulation in the sense that one can never *see* an intention; it has to be inferred from other cues.

The theory-of-mind argument is often backed up by presuppositions about so-called mental modules. Discussions on mental modularity mainly take place in cognitive science and evolutionary psychology. Especially theorists working in the latter field often argue that the mind consists of modules or psychological devices which have specialized in solving specific cognitive problems. The ability to interpret other minds is supposedly an "interpretative competence (…) dissociated from other aspects of human cognitions," as Sterelny (2003, 211) summarizes the modular view. Thus, there is a theory of mind module that is *innate* in the human mind. The modular character implies that it is "encapsulated" from our other cognitive functions: it is a domain-specific device for interpreting the actions and attitudes of others which, through a developmental process, enables one also to interpret one's own mind. There are studies indicating that both of these interpretative abilities are lacking in autistic persons, thus showing that autists are in this sense "mind-blind" (Baron-Cohen 1995). If this is indeed the case, then it would seem to corroborate Mead's line of thinking in which self-consciousness – being an object to oneself – is an ability that develops through taking the attitudes of others towards and into oneself.

However, there are other, competing explanations for our social abilities. As an alternative to the module view, Sterelny (2003, 215) offers the so-called simulation theory. According to this theory, "we predict and interpret the behavior of others by using our own decision-making procedures as a model" (ibid.). This theory has the advantage of fitting the phenomenology of agency, as we often seem to be interpreting others by projecting ourselves into their shoes, rather than the other way round (ibid., 216). This can be a fitting characterization of the way sympathetic reactions work once these reactions have developed. However, this is not necessarily a description of the *development* of selfhood. Even if we agree with Sterelny's argument, we can limit its relevance to the functioning of a fully developed selfhood. Thus its development can still be a process in which we learn that others react to our actions in different ways and these reactions cause us to objectify our actions – and, eventually, ourselves. And what is even more important, Mead's view is *not* dependent on the modular view of the theory of mind being literally true. In fact, the modular view sounds a little too nativistic from a Meadian perspective since Mead underscores the complex interaction of the actor and its environment rather than the independent and "native" role of psychological factors.

In addition, speaking of a *theory* of mind can give a too intellectual picture of our mental abilities. The ability to share attention with other people is probably rooted in our brains. This suggestion has been made by Gallese (2006) who is one of the proponents of the importance of mirror neurons (see also Iacoboni 2008). These neurons refer to the finding that when we observe someone doing something, the same neurons "fire" (that is, get activated) in our brains that would fire if we were to do that same thing ourselves. For example, when one sees someone drinking a glass of water, it seems that our brains instinctively prepare us for doing that activity ourselves. Thus one could argue that perceiving is about acting – even at the neuronal level (cf. Noë 2004). Gallese (2005) argues that rather than having a theory of other minds, we "attune" to the intentions of others through embodied simulation. If this is true then the only ones needing a theory of other minds are probably autists because it is "the only compensating strategy available in the absence of more elementary and basic cognitive skills enabling a direct experiential take on the world of others" (ibid., 22). This might sound like a refutation of Mead's views but I do not think that Mead's insights are necessarily dependent on the theory of mind view being true; rather, they are compatible with Gallese's arguments as well. One could even claim that Gallese's arguments seem to point to a very Meadian conclusion: intersubjectivity is very basic attitude which comes to us – literally – naturally.[14] It is exhibited in a sense of being part of a "we," of sharing intentionality by default (see Tomasello 2008).

In the original article (see chapter 2), I argued that other animals react to members of their species and are capable of rudimentary co-operation. This argument finds corroboration in a book by Tomasello (2008). For example, chimpanzees (our cousins) also co-operate to some extent but they do so from an individualistic perspective (to get something they personally want). In addition, they are able to understand things from their own perspective and from the perspective of others, but what is lacking is a "bird's-eye view" which is an essential feature of humanity. Such a view entails that one understands "the joint goal [of co-operation] and complementary roles all in a single representational format" (ibid., 179). The "birds-eye view" could be another name for Mead's generalized other because both concepts underscore the ability to see the roles of oneself and the roles of others from an objective perspective which transcends a purely individualistic outlook.

---

14 This conclusion is drawn by Franks (2010) in his book *Neurosociology*.

Institutionalization as Habitualization

Chapter 3 is entitled *Not by Rules or Choice Alone: A Pragmatist Critique of Institution Theories in Economics and Sociology*. Here the background assumption is that social structures can fruitfully be conceptualized as institutions. First, a general classification of different institution theories is presented, originally employed by W. Richard Scott, and followed by the argument that there is a need for a habitual theory of institutions due to problems in "standard" institution theories. The different institution theories are called regulative, normative and discursive theories, to which I have added the notion of habitual theories. Regulative views are especially in vogue in economics since they often posit an actor relying on calculative rationality; that is, they do not alter the basic tenet of economics which says that on the basis of our preferences we aim to achieve the largest amount of utility with the help of calculations. However, the so-called New Institutionalists (or Neoinstitutionalists) in economics have argued that we always act within institutional constraints. For example, Douglass C. North, a famous proponent of institutional thought in economics, has maintained that institutions are akin to the rules of games, constraining our possible actions. As constraints, institutions can either be formal or informal. Formal constraints are usually consciously devised whereas informal constraints are more subtle conventions.

Even though regulative institutionalists also discuss the informal aspects of institutions they nevertheless tend to stress that institutions are the outcome of rational calculations because it is rational for actors to follow certain institutional regulations. What makes it rational is especially the existence of sanctions. This is not the traditional way of looking at things in sociology. Sociologists have often underscored the normatively binding character of institutions and this position can be labeled normative institutionalism. In such a view, society is based on a consensus on values from which more specific norms can be drawn. These norms are internalized in socialization and they "tell" us how to behave in various situations. Thus, norms are the main element of social order. Normative institutionalists tend not to discuss themes relating to the interpretation of institutions. This issue, however, is the basis of discursive theories of institutions. These theories argue that institutions are knowledge-like typifications. Despite the best of intentions, none of the above theories really succeeds in relating institutions to action.

Habitual institutionalism, as I call it, accounts for institutions in terms of established and prevalent social dispositions that structure our social interactions. The germs of this theory can be found in the work of Thorstein Veblen, especially in his critical writings on the methodology of economics. Veblen's institutional views are based on pragmatist ideas. A contemporary representative of habitual institutionalism is the economist Geoffrey M. Hodgson (although he does not use my label). His ideas on the evolution of institutions are presented in this chapter but a critical stance is taken towards his tendency of defining institutions through rules because institutions are not always connected with rules. Accordingly, habitual action is the most basic aspect of institutional reproduction. The definition of institution that I use states that institutions are established and prevalent social dispositions that structure social (inter)action. Other institutional theories highlight many important aspects of institutions but the presuppositions of these other institutional theories should be reconciled with those of habitual institutionalism rather than the other way around.

Classifying Institutions

As mentioned, I take my cue from W. Richard Scott's classificatory scheme (Scott 2001; 2008). However, Scott's classification of institutional theories differs somewhat from my usage; there are the familiar regulative and normative theories but the third theory-type I call cultural-cognitive, not discursive. In addition, habitual theories do not figure as a class of their own in Scott's work. His idea is that his classification can be used as a way of discerning institutional "pillars." By "pillars" he means that one can discuss different *aspects* of institutions. Thus, rather than being mutually exclusive, these theories point out certain elements of institutions. The reason for the renaming of the cultural-cognitive "discursive" is that I want to highlight the fact that Scott's cultural-cognitive theories are theories that mainly (although not exclusively) concentrate on discursive aspects. There is all the more reason for making this distinction since the habitual aspects of action are not necessarily discursive. Of course, phenomena having to do with cultural-cognitive issues – cultural representations, for example – are often also habitual, but the theoretical traditions that Scott refers to with the cultural-cognitive label (for example, DiMaggio and Powell) are such that they tend to think of habitual issues as being mainly discursive, at least in origin.[15] This differs from the pragmatist usage of the idea of habits and therefore there is reason enough for making the distinction. However, if one wants to avoid giving birth to yet another label, the alternative would be to redescribe the contents of the cultural-cognitive pillar so that it comprises habitual theories as well.

The more serious question is whether this classification is able to capture the gamut of different institutional theories. This question is even more pressing if one claims that institutions are the same thing as social structures and therefore this classification applies, *mutatis mutandis*, to all theories of structures as well. The answer is that it is naturally possible to think of theories that do not fit so well into this scheme.

---

15 In such a view, discursive factors can "sink" below the level of consciousness as they are habitualized but the basic form of meaning is discursive. Thus, there are good reasons for making the distinction between discursive and habitual theories.

For example, does Foucauldian theory fit into this picture? It is not so much a theory of institutions, at least not explicitly, but also Foucault has a theory of social structures (although it is somewhat implicit). In his theory, structures are discursive but not merely so. A major theme in Foucauldian circles has concerned the relationship between discursive factors and practice (Hall 2001). One could argue therefore that Foucault presents a theory in which social structures are mainly discursive – structural elements can be seen, foe example, in documents produced by doctors and other agents of so-called biopower. However, to have effects on anything, that is, to really become social structures, these discursive factors should be seen in people's practices. Thus, Foucault's theories are situated somewhere between the discursive and the habitual but in a manner that places too little emphasis on the habitual because he does not have an explicit theory of action.

The placement of other authors and their theories in this scheme could also be debated. For example, if, again, we think of Scott's classification as a classification of social structures rather than just theories of institutions, then is there a place for Pierre Bourdieu in this scheme? I think that the answer would come close to the one that I just gave in relation to Foucault: Bourdieu is somewhere in between discursive and habitual theories: unlike Foucault he has an explicit theory of action. Both of these authors aim to uncover hidden laws of societal power in a very critical manner, which is something that pragmatist theories do not usually do. I will get back to this issue while discussing Bourdieu at more length. Here it suffices to say that there probably are also many other writers whose ideas might not fit so well into this scheme. For example, some authors working within the framework of rational choice theory are building synthetic theories which incorporate diverse phenomena, including issues of identity and even habituality (see Macy 1997). However, my usage of Scott's classifications is meant to be taken as analytical distinctions rather than as an all-encompassing meta-theory of institutional views.

The Nature of Institutions

It has always been a commonplace to criticize economist's views of action in sociology. However, this criticism has traditionally met with surprisingly little concern. The answer given by economists to this criticism has often been that economics deals with models, not with realistic depictions of human action. It is of course all too easy to mix the model with reality, an issue that I discuss in the context of Bourdieu's work, but one can still argue that the whole point of using models is to be aware of their simplified nature. For example, a map of New York gives a simplified picture of the city with that name. However, there is a point in using a map if one compares it to the actual city. One could argue that too often economists are not interested in the relationship between the model and reality – and, if they were, they would probably have to do some serious editing to their models.

Economists certainly get one thing right: they never lose sight of action. Sociologists too often think that social structures somehow hover above our heads, independently of action, but determining that action. If action is not the starting point for a theory of structures, it is quite difficult to explain the relationship between action and structures. All institutional theories underscore that a certain amount of stability is a necessary condition for the existence of institutions. For example, one probably should not call a particular fashion trend an institution due to its very provisional character, although fashion itself is surely an institution. The habitual foundation of institutions means that in familiar environments people generally tend to react in ways that have "worked" before. The *environment* of action should be conceptualized very broadly: it consists of other actors, different kinds of artifacts and material instruments, buildings and sometimes even the inner "environment" of the actor (the feedback given by his or her inner organs). Quite often it is the case that only some (or one) of these aspects of the environment is in the forefront, but that does not mean that the other aspects would somehow disappear from the scene altogether.

Even though a certain amount of stability is an essential feature of institutions, institutions are always prone to change. In fact, and despite the stability required by the concept, change is ever-present in relation to institutions because of the processual character of action. This also means that often the most interesting cases are those where habits are under reconstruction due to changes in the institutional environment. It can also happen that actors actively try to initiate crises in their habits themselves; for example, science is an institution that often tries to do precisely this, for example, with incentives that encourage calling into question the results of previous research.

One thing that I do not dwell on is the distinction between the way in which institutions are born and the way in which they are maintained once in place. One does not always have to make this distinction for the simple reason that in many cases it can be difficult to discern the exact places and dates of birth. However, the mechanisms of institutional birth and maintenance are not necessarily the same thing either. The issue is implicit in the table of institution theories (see chapter 3), where it is viewed as one of three different bases: those of compliance, order and legitimacy. For example, in the case of habitual theories, shared dispositions are the reason why one engages in joint activities with others in the first place (*the basis of compliance*). Once these ways of acting have been going on for awhile, they become taken for granted (*the basis of order*) and make one a proficient actor in the world (*the basis of legitimacy*). Naturally, these distinctions are more or less analytical because in reality these issues are always tied together: sharing a disposition and being proficient in doing a related act makes it easy to take the habit in question for granted.

For some social scientists, referring to evolutionary theory is like showing a red rag to a bull. Therefore it is probably in order to emphasize that Geoffrey Hodgson's usage of evolutionary theory in the context of the concept of institution is not a form of biological reductionism. Hodgson consistently argues that the evolution of institutions takes place on another level than biological evolution (Hodgson 2001; 2004; 2006). Thus, a discussion of institutional evolution has its own set of research questions and these are not the same as those in biology. Hodgson's evolutionary analogy is based on the supposition that institutions have similar systemic aspects as organisms have. That is, they have some sorts of borders and, as open systems, they interact with their environments and are dependent on them. The systemic nature of institutions also implies that they sometimes seem like actors to us, as they are not dependent on any particular person's wishes or wants. However, it is likely that only some institutions would actually fit with the definition of an actual system. For example, many organizations spring to mind because they have actual borders (who belongs to the organization, what the organization owns, etc.) and they also have explicit goals and official positions (see Hodgson 2010). Clearly many institutions lack these characteristics which is an issue that Hodgson does not reflect on as much as he could. Thus, when one speaks of institutions as systems, then the reference is clearly to such institutions that are organizations.[16]

Hodgson has called his perspective universal or generalized Darwinism (see, e.g., Aldrich et al. 2008; Hodgson & Knudsen 2007). Such a perspective argues that while "there is not a fierce life-and-death struggle between rival customs or institutions, some explanation is required of why some enjoy greater longevity than others" (ibid., 585). Complete identity with biological evolution is not called for as Hodgson and his colleagues explain: "the idea of generalizing Darwinism is not about analogies and does not depend on the proposition that the detailed mechanisms of social and biological evolution are similar" (ibid., 591-592). The detailed mechanisms, then, do not have to be similar, but the general features certainly have to be similar enough for there to be any point in generalizing Darwinism in such a manner. Hodgson maintains that institutional evolution can be explained by referring to selection pressures, just as in the case of biological evolution. However, this assumption provides only a "'meta-theory', an overarching framework wherein theorists place particular explanations" (ibid., 585). The only requirement in applying evolutionary theory to institutions is that there is some variation, a mechanism of "heritability" and some differential selection of institutions due to their environments (or more precisely, due to their interaction with their environment).

That there is variation between institutions is an undeniable fact. The controversial issues are thus whether one can also identify something akin to heritability and

---

16 As is well known, Niklas Luhmann's system's theory has discussed these issues at length. However, Luhmannian themes are beyond the scope of this book.

selection in the case of institutions. Hodgson's candidates for the mechanisms of heritability are – not surprisingly – habits and routines. Habits can be shared and they are often learned from other people, although not necessarily through explicit instruction. Learning processes, can, in general, be either vertical or horizontal; that is, one can learn from one's parents or from one's peers. In this regard habits certainly differ from genes since peer-to-peer gene-transfer is not possible (at least in the case of humans). However, it might still be useful to think of habits as the unit – or, at least, one of the units – of the inheritance of culture. This process is not necessarily opposed to biological inheritance but, rather, biological and cultural ways of inheriting information are probably in complex interaction with each other. Thus, they coevolve (see Richerson & Boyd 2005, Ridley 2004).[17] Nevertheless, analytically we have to be able to separate these two ways of mediating information: the biological and the cultural. If heritability can be conceptualized as taking place through habits (although with certain reservations), what about the process of selection?

One objection that is often made against Darwinism is that it presumably seems to argue for the survival of the strongest and for some sort of optimal results. Survival of the fittest is indeed what Darwinism argues for but the fittest are not necessarily the strongest (whatever this might mean in practice). Fitness is a relative concept – relative to the environment. For example, in the case of humans biological evolution has favored the ability for intersubjectivity, that is, it has been selected by the environment (that is, other people have played a major role in it), which has enabled co-operation in ways not encountered among other species. In addition, the results of biological evolution are rarely optimal; rather, they are good enough. One thing that puts limits to any fantasies of optimality is that evolution builds on pre-existing foundations and cannot start from scratch. For example, the spine is better suited for walking on all fours but it is all we had when the ancestors of humans started walking on their hind legs. It is good enough for this purpose but anything but optimal (witness the prevalence of backache). Also in the case of institutions one does not have to think that they are optimal but good enough in relation to their environments (other institutions and material aspects) and in relation to their own history which places constraints as well. As mentioned before, existing habits are the basis on which one can envision other ways of doing things.

One major issue still needs to be discussed: the implications of thinking in terms of populations. Sociologists have been very fond of the idea of ideal types, as advocated by Max Weber. Ideal types tend to cut variation out of the picture as they focus on

---

17 Jablonka and Lamb (2005) have argued that there are actually four different kinds of inheritance: genetic, epigenetic (non-DNA but at the level of cells), behavioral and symbolic. In Jablonka and Lamb's scheme, Hodgson's habitual inheritance would take place both at the behavioral and symbolic levels.

the essential parts of any phenomenon. Darwinism, however, is an example of population thinking and, thus, it underscores the importance of variation. Populations consist of entities that vary on a certain scale (or scales) and this random variation is one of the major sources of novelty. For example, in the case of habits, the emergence of novel ways of doing things can be a source of institutional change. However, variation cannot be just presumed, it has to be explained. Biological evolution has its mutations but in social evolution one can argue that – and this is an argument that has not been proposed by Hodgson – learning is always based on relevance, that is, on our existing biological and habitual dispositions, and this means that we are more sensitive to pick out certain habits than others (or certain bits of habits). Sperber (1996) has argued along similar lines when he criticizes the so-called meme idea which relies too much on the assumption that cultural "units" would get copied with the same accuracy as genes (excluding occasional mutations). Such accuracy is not possible because the relevant aspects are the ones that are favored in learning.

Cultural units, habits in my analysis, are not exact copies and therefore there is probably more variation in the case of social evolution. Thus, habits exhibit variation and this can be a source of variation for institutions as well and, in addition, there is likely to be variation *among* institutions. This is where things get complicated because the environment of institutions is comprised of other similar institutions (e.g., different marriage institutions) and other, different sorts of institutions (e.g., institutions related to economic markets). Sometimes there can be an element of interpenetration which means that institutions can be interlocked to such an extent that it is difficult to tell them apart. This can also mean that there is some functionality among them which is, of course, an issue put forth by Parsonian functionalist sociology. However, contrary to Parsonian views, I do not think that functionality is a conceptual issue. Rather, it is an open issue whether institutions exhibit functionality in relation to other institutions. Thus, it should be left for empirical research to see whether this is the case. Hodgson's insights into social evolution seem interesting and worth pursuing and they are certainly in the pragmatist, Veblenian spirit. However, it must also be stressed that conceptualizing institutions through social habits is not necessarily dependent on generalizing Darwinism in the way that Hodgson does it.

One perplexing issue concerns the relationship between the concepts of "institution" and "social structure". As implied previously, these concepts can be mentioned in the same breath because both refer to the structural aspects of society. Institutions can be defined as established and prevalent social dispositions that structure social (inter)action. If one also includes all the material arrangements related to institutions in this definition then one should have something synonymous to a social structure. Hodgson (2006, 138) offers an argument where structures have to do with social relations and institutions, more specifically, with rules. Thus, structures consist of all social relations, whereas institutions are those relations that have a rule-like character.

For example, it seems evident that quite formal rules are involved in organizations. However, the real issue is whether it is wise to connect institutions with rules by way of definition – and even if it were wise, do all social structures have rule-like characteristics. To be precise, Hodgson actually says that institutions come down to rules, not to rule-*like* issues. I am afraid that the linkage with actual rules runs the risk of seeing institutions in a too formal light: either there has to be an actual, existing codified rule, or we must postulate it into existence. The latter procedure can work in some cases but not necessarily always. A tentative solution could be that rather than defining institutions as rules, one can argue that they are social dispositions that usually have rule-like characters. These characters can, of course, exhibit themselves in actual rules. Defining institutions with the help of dispositions has the additional advantage that it fits well with the pragmatist view which stresses habits as the origin of our social formations (rather than discursive factors). However, I will not object if someone wants to define institutions through rules – if it is added that rules refer only to regularities of action. Some regularities of social action are "only" habitual dispositions and get a voicing in cases where their self-evident character is in doubt. For example, there is no official rule saying that technical occupations are only for men but it is probably due to habitual reasons that men are overrepresented in these professions (of course, there might also be a biological basis for this empirical fact).

Stressing the dispositional and habitual nature of institutions enables one to analyze institutional aspects in all cases where the required stability and conformity of action is present. Some commentators have argued that such an institutional conception is too broad (see Fleetwood 2008). A more narrow definition is certainly in order in some cases but this issue depends on the research question at hand. For example, Tomasello (2009, 55, 59) argues that in addition to the physical and social worlds also inhabited by other apes, only humans live in an institutional world with its "public social norms and the assignment of deontic status to institutional roles." In such a context (drawing a distinction between humans and other apes), it certainly is in order to link institutions mainly with norms. However, I do not think that there are any problems in an extensive institutional conception because institutionalization happens to be a – or even *the* – foundational feature of social reality. This is due to the fact that we are not inventing our habits anew all the time; rather, we encounter familiar social situations and act accordingly.

It is in order to combat a purely discursive aspect view of society that I want to underscore the essential link between habits and dispositions (rather than habits and rules). In practice, it is probably often the case that institutions are intertwined with rules and norms. Furthermore, referring to habits should not act as a catch word that ends all discussion. In addition, more precise definitions are called for if one wants to operationalize this concept empirically. I suggest that habits could be studied, for example, through routines or by taking the essential role that metaphorical thought plays in our lives. Routines are probably the most studied aspect in relation to habits but they are often approached from a psychological perspective (see, e.g., Wood et al. 2002). This is quite natural since routines are indeed a psychological phenomenon. However, they are not exclusively related to psychology because they can have effects on the societal level. Thus, when a large number of people act according to routine habits, then those not doing so are faced with a social structure. As we all know, it takes a special effort to deviate from such collective routines; even spelling out the existence of such a routine can be met with disapproval. However, identifying habits with routines faces the danger of making them too thing-like. The pragmatist way of using the concept, after all, emphasizes the processual character of habits and the way in which they interact with conscious control.

In addition to routines, I mention the possibility of operationalizing habits via metaphorical thought. In recent cognitive science there has been an upsurge in research into metaphorical thought. The book by Lakoff and Johnson which started the interest, *Metaphors We Live By*, was published in 1980 but the broader implications of their work are truly fleshed out in a later book, *Philosophy in the Flesh* (1999). These authors argue that "reason has grown out of sensory and motor systems and (…) it still uses those systems or structures developed from them" (Lakoff & Johnson 1999, 43). One of their major claims is that even our abstract thought is based on metaphors that take their cue, that is, their source, from bodily aspects. For example, understanding the metaphor that "more is up" entails a sensorimotor experience of something being added on top of something else (or into something else in the case of fluids) (ibid., 51). Lakoff and Johnson do not discuss habits explicitly but their basic assumption is that the mind is embodied, which is implied with the concept of habit.[18] The usage of bodily metaphors is often unconscious and thus I am proposing that habits can be conceptualized according to the framework given by Lakoff and Johnson.

Habitus and Habits

The fourth chapter takes up the issue of action and structures in the context of Pierre Bourdieu's thought and it entitled *Uneasy Bedfellows or Natural Allies? Bourdieu and Pragmatism*. Bourdieu's term "habitus" refers to a system of dispositions which structure social fields. In essence, habitus is the subjective side of social positions. It has sometimes been argued that habitus comes close to the idea of habits, as professed by pragmatists. Quite surprisingly, there are no systematic treatments of this issue to

---

18 Johnson has explicitly discussed the relationship between pragmatism and cognitive science in general. His conclusion is that pragmatism can provide "the larger philosophical framework for appreciating and criticizing the assumptions and results of the cognitive sciences" (Johnson 2006, 376).

be found in social theory. This chapter is an attempt to remedy this deficiency. First, there are points of convergence in Bourdieu's arguments and in the pragmatist vision: a stress on the practical and habitual nature of our actions instead of an intellectualist mindset. However, there are also clear differences: Bourdieu mainly discusses his concept of habitus in relation to socioeconomic differences whereas the habits of pragmatists relate to all regularities in action. In addition, pragmatists discuss the role of creativity at more length. Even more importantly, Bourdieu is first and foremost a theorist of the way in which we differentiate ourselves from others while pragmatism (especially Mead's version) is interested in such sociality which does not preclude identifying with others – even if they differ from us in their habits. However, these differences between Bourdieu and pragmatism can be taken as complementary perspectives rather than irreconcilable conflicts.

Bourdieu and His Many Critics

The difficulty with discussing Bourdieu's work – or the work of any author that has attracted so much attention – is naturally the fact that there are so many commentaries and topics of discussion related to his ideas. This abundance of commentaries is usually a sign of the fruitfulness of ideas and this certainly applies in Bourdieu's case. However, it is not only fruitfulness of ideas that has produced much discussion in relation to Bourdieu. One factor generating diverse opinions is that Bourdieu was sometimes somewhat vague in his argumentation. In addition, although there is continuity in all of Bourdieu's work, his interests and opinions did change with time. For example, the role that public politics had in his late years has aroused discussion whether this public and political role constituted a break with his former professional status (see Frangie 2009). Naturally, I am not able to discuss the whole of Bourdieu's career or all aspects of his thinking, and fortunately, there are good and multifaceted commentaries around (e.g. Calhoun et al. 1993, Swartz 1997, Shusterman 1999).

Some people might argue that rather than being action-centered, Bourdieu's framework is about spatial relations. Bourdieu himself certainly emphasized this point: his "notion of *space* contains, in itself, the principle of a *relational* understanding of the social world" (Bourdieu 1998, 31). A relational understanding is one in which things "exist and subsist in and through *difference*; that is they occupy *relative positions* in a space of relations" (ibid.). These citations contain an important message as they point to Bourdieu's theory as relational and positional. However, such a theory can at the same time have action at its centre and as its starting point.

Some commentators have noticed that Bourdieu can be used to underscore aspects of status. For example, Gross (2003) interprets Bourdieu as a theorist of status-based intellectual choice. He argues that for Bourdieu "individual thinkers tend to be drawn toward the intellectual approaches associated with their current institutional locations, or with the institutional locations to which they aspire" (ibid., 54). The effect this has is that "positions in social space and positions in the space of ideas" (ibid.) establish a homology; that is, they tend to correlate with each other. What this means in practice is that in the case of cultural tastes, for example, one's socioeconomic background correlates with the tastes that one happens to have. In addition, Gross sees Bourdieu as arguing that the search for better status positions is our main motive in any field of life.

This interest in socioeconomic background has led some commentators to argue that, in essence, Bourdieu presents us with a theory of social classes. Sweetman (2003, 532) is a case in point when he says that Bourdieu is discussing embodied class-culture. However, not all authors would agree with Sweetman. For example, Rahkonen (1999, 16) argues that Bourdieu's is a "sociology of domination or symbolic power, and not so much, as every now and then Bourdieu's work has been (mis)interpreted, a sociology of class." According to Rahkonen, Bourdieu "is more interested in elaborating relationships of domination or power than developing any class theory proper" (ibid.). It is true, as Rahkonen remarks, that Bourdieu's class concepts are not that refined; it is the basic three-fold distinction into upper, middle and proletarian classes. Thus, Bourdieu does indeed seem to be more interested in the ways that classifying people have effects on social life rather than on social classes as such. These facts can be taken as indications that he does not present a proper theory of social classes. However, it cannot be denied that Bourdieu lays a great deal of emphasis on socioeconomic background and especially on education. This emphasis is sometimes laid at the expense of other important factors. The education of one's parents and of oneself is certainly important as a background variable in all social research. Nonetheless, there are other factors that have to be taken into account when studying taste, for example. In a study by Purhonen et al. (2009, 47), it was found that "age and especially gender proved to be at least as important as education in explaining musical and literary taste patterns."

Some critics have argued that Bourdieu is too close to the utilitarian picture of society as an entity based on utility calculations. For example, Heiskala (2003, appendix 5) has claimed that Bourdieu is guilty of the sin of economism; that is, he explains the working of society with economic metaphors. Lebaron (2003: 551-2) has discerned two different lines in these critiques of economism directed at Bourdieu. The first argues that Bourdieu presents a neoclassical vision of society (based on selfish interests), whereas the other disagrees with Bourdieu's use of economic analogies as a form of Marxist determinism. Lebaron's own judgment is that Bourdieu does indeed use economic models but he uses them as metaphors, not as literal devices. Naturally, there is nothing wrong with using metaphors as such – in fact, they are an inevitable part of even our most abstract ideas (Lakoff & Johnson 1999). As Lebaron (2003:

552) suggests, the real critical issue is therefore whether Bourdieu's metaphors are too limited for their intended use. Joas and Knöbl (2009, 384) argue that "like *all* utilitarians, he [Bourdieu] continues to adhere to the notion that people (consciously or non-consciously) always pursue their interests." Action is based on strategies that are used to "improve the player's position within a particular field or at least to uphold the status quo" (ibid.). Joas and Knöbl conclude that Bourdieu's theory is an original mixture of utilitarian thinking, conflict theory and Marxism.

I argue that in some ways these metaphors can indeed be too limited – if we use them as the only model for general theory of action and social structures. It also seems that Bourdieu was not cautious enough because sometimes one gets the impression that he tends not to see the metaphorical nature of his basic vocabulary (e.g., "cultural *capital*"). At the same time, it should be clear that Bourdieu does not advocate a picture of action as consciously rational, which is the basic tenet of many forms of rational choice theory. In his own words, Bourdieu's way of using the notion of interest was actually "a deliberate and provisional reductionism that allows me [i.e., Bourdieu] to import the materialist mode of questioning into the cultural sphere from which it was expelled, historically, when the modern view of art was invented and the field of cultural production won its autonomy" (Bourdieu & Wacquant 1992, 116). One can interpret Bourdieu as presenting us with a model which should be judged by the fruitfulness of its results and not by its presuppositions.

Social Reproduction: What is it all About?

My basic tenet is that Bourdieu and pragmatism are theoretically quite close to each other. I am aware that this is not the first time this resemblance is noticed (see, e.g., Aboulafia 1999; Colapietro 2004a) but previous commentators have not really elaborated on the issue of how these theories relate to one another. This resemblance can best be captured by looking at what both have to say on issues of action and social structures.

Thus, Bourdieu and pragmatists (especially Mead and Dewey) underscore the way in which habitual action is the key to social reproduction. Bourdieu's concept of habitus is related to socioeconomic factors whereas the habitual dimension of pragmatists refers to habituality in general. There is a case to be made for the latter position because not even all those habits that relate to societal reproduction are necessarily based on socioeconomic divisions; many of them naturally are, but it is an empirical issue and not a theoretical one to decide which of them strictly speaking have a socioeconomic basis. I am not saying that social differentiation would not matter or that no hierarchical social positions would exist. Both of these phenomena are major parts of all human societies. For example, in a recent book it is argued that "the most powerful sources of stress affecting health seem to fall into three intensely social categories: low social status, lack of friends, and stress in early life" (Wilkinson & Pickett 2010, 39). Thus, issues related to social positions (low social status) affect our lives very concretely through health issues, for example. These authors also suggest that the importance of one's social position is more important in unequal settings: "Instead of accepting each other as equal on the basis of our common humanity as we might in more equal settings, getting the measure of each other becomes more important as status differences widen" (ibid., 43).[19]

Accordingly, there is some data that suggests that the ability to see things from other's perspective and to feel empathy are decreasing (at least among American college students; see Konrath et al. 2010). One could then argue that Mead's vision of a generalized other becoming a "universalized other" – seeing our common humanity – first requires that our social positions are equal enough to begin with. In a very divided society it might be difficult to overcome the divisions – even in one's head. This could, then, be a major criticism of Mead: he does not see the harsh realities of the world. However, one can also read his work as a general description about the formation of our selfhood through social relations. This description is apt even in unequal societies because the basic building blocks of selfhood do not differ very much. In addition, Mead's view of universalizing our generalized others can also act as a regulative ideal. In such a role, it can direct our search for more inclusive social identities and for more equal social settings.

When discussing Bourdieu's concept of habitus, one should remember that habitus is primarily related to a certain field(s); habitus incorporates social biography, and the field is its objective, structural counterpart. Thus our dispositions, embodied in the habitus and taking the form of different capitals, are "acquired through learning processes associated with protracted dealings with the regularities of the field [in question]" (Bourdieu 2005, 8-9). By way of definition, Bourdieu said, for example, that a field is "a network, or a configuration, of objective relations between positions" (Bourdieu & Wacquant 1992, 97). These positions are occasions for struggles for the particular capital accumulated in the fields. In short, the amount of capital one has determines one's position in a field, and power tends to accumulate in certain positions. In addition, there often is a homology between positions in different fields. Thus, a particular position in, say, the cultural field can also indicate a comparable position in some other field. The limits of fields are defined by the types of capital characteristic of them. For example, in the scientific field, it is scientific authority or competence that one struggles for and that defines one's position. The picture Bourdieu paints is one of relentless competition and struggle over social positions.

---

19 The problem with Wilkinson and Pickett's thesis is that they treat equality only as an issue of income distribution (however, they do so self-consciously). This would be unacceptable to a Bourdieusian and to followers of Amartya Sen.

Leaving this competitive aspect aside for now, it could be argued that Bourdieu's field is close to the concept of institution. After all, both concepts refer to the phenomenon of societal reproduction. The concept of institution was not totally unknown to Bourdieu; he argued, for example, that "the *habitus* is what enables the institution to attain full realization" (Bourdieu 1990, 57). He also discussed institution as a process in which social properties are assigned "in a way that makes them seem like properties of natural nature" (Bourdieu 1991, 118). This "naturalization" is certainly one of the main effects of institutions, and is the result of habitualization. Thus, institutions are based on such habits that are, to a certain extent, shared by the parties concerned (they allow for participation in common activities). Swartz (1997, 120) has argued that field analysis is actually Bourdieu's version of institutional theory. According to Swartz, Bourdieu prefers the concept of fields to institutions because he wants to highlight conflicts and also situations that are only weakly institutionalized. There is certainly the danger of seeing institutions in functionalist terms, but functionalism is not a necessary corollary of institutional theory. In fact, one could even argue that the concept of institution can be approached as a more general category, whereas fields are particular kinds of institutions, namely those which are hierarchical and more or less organized, with easily discernible social positions that are prone to competition. Institutions are more general regularities of action and thus not always arenas of such competition which is characteristic of fields, but this does not mean that they are functional havens of order, either. They can just as well be the cumulative effects of habitual ways of acting in social situations that are often repeated.

Bourdieusians would probably argue – if they accepted fields to institutions in the first place – that institutions are always hierarchical and related to socioeconomic differences. However, this argument is an over-simplification. There are habitual aspects of our conduct that contribute to the reproduction of social structures without necessarily contributing to hierarchical, socioeconomic relations. One could also argue that even in the case of field-like institutions, there are habits that contribute to their social reproduction without, strictly speaking, being part of a habitus. It is simply unconvincing to assume that field-related habits always take the form of strategic struggles over some kind of capital. If we take the example of the intellectual or the academic field, some of our habits certainly take this form, but not all habits because some of them are related to our self-concepts in which narrative continuity can override concerns about academic position and status (see Gross 2008).

One issue that has drawn considerable attention is Bourdieu's political involvement in the late phase of his career. If one sees Bourdieu's theory as advocating a quite deterministic picture of the reproduction of society – a particular socioeconomic background produces a similar socioeconomic position – it can be difficult to argue that there is any place left for political agency. This dilemma is diagnosed, for example, by Joas and Knöbl (2009). Bourdieu's theory is a critical theory and the dilemma of freedom of action is faced by all such theories. However, other authors have been more optimistic about the potential of Bourdieu's theory for social change. Frangie (2009, 216) explains that the link between Bourdieu's "theories and politics, or his academic and public postures, is his analysis of the logic of fields, endowing his political involvement with a reflexive dimension." However, one might still conclude that the concept of habitus "introduces a significant amount of skepticism regarding the emancipatory potential of knowledge," as Frangie (ibid., 217) acknowledges. The key to the possible transformatory potential of Bourdieusian politics is the way in which reflecting on the principles of social reproduction can lead to the transformations of one's habitus. Thus, it is through socio-analysis – analyzing the social factors that have made us who we are – that one can claim some amount of freedom in relation to one's background. This is the only way that we can escape, at least to some extent, from the domination of the logic of the fields.

Archer (2007, 41) has argued that Bourdieu nevertheless seriously downplays the role of reflexivity, and this fault results from a "central conflation." This concept refers to a view where action and social structures are mutually constitutive entities; they are on the same level, so to speak.[20] Because he is guilty of central conflation, "Bourdieu's agents do not confront circumstances, but are an integral part of them" (ibid., 42). Circumstances are thus always an embodied part of us in the form of our habitus. This supposedly means that we fail to recognize the habit to which our habitus corresponds, possibly excluding some situations in which there is a mismatch between habitus and circumstances. However, Archer is, again, on a mission to underscore the role of reflexivity and for that reason is not willing to give Bourdieu due credit. It can be admitted that Bourdieu does not treat issues of emergence with systematic intent but this does not mean that he has no place for reflexivity. There is a place for it, even though a smaller one than Mead reserves for it. The continuous dialectic of the "I" and the "me" therefore gives a more nuanced picture of reflexivity and the way in which there is a permanent place for creativity in human action.

To conclude, I want to stress that an analysis of power relations and socioeconomic factors is certainly one of the main concerns of social theory and sociology but it is not the only topic of interest. One can think of empirical examples in which the analysis of more general habits is more to the point (see the chapter for an empirical example). In addition, an overemphasis of the role of power relations can also be a real problem: sociology should not become an advocate for parochial interests. Sociology, as a representative of the very fallible but objective inquiry called science, should not forget the general issues that connect us. Haack (2008, 34-35) is to the point in this quotation: "As the stress on interests of this or that class or category of person has

---

20 Anthony Giddens' conception of the duality of action and structures is a famous example of such a conflatory view.

waxed, our sense of our common humanity and our appreciation of individual differences has waned, until we are in danger of forgetting that fallible inquiry – the ragged, untidy process of groping for, and sometimes grasping, something of how the world is – is a *human* thing, not a white male thing."

Pragmatism and Social Philosophy

The last chapter of the book comes closest to issues of social politics or social philosophy and is entitled *Integrating the Capabilities Approach with Pragmatism*. The capabilities approach has been associated with the name of Amartya Sen, for example, and it underscores problems inhering in economistic ways of evaluating social development. Sen argues that the main indicator of development should be people's capabilities rather than economic growth as such. Capabilities refer to the actual abilities that people have to achieve certain things that are part of the well-being of society (these things can differ in different societies). Sen's argument is also useful in the field of social theory because after the so-called cultural turn many have shunned mentioning the possibility that there could be development in social issues. However, Sen's argument has some theoretical problems. First, Sen emphasizes active agency but his theory of action is too passive. Second, his theory cannot adequately confront the problem of relativism. In addition, Sen's discussion lacks a theory of the role of the public. These problems can be tackled with the help of some pragmatist ideas. Thus, it is possible to postulate an action-based, socially constituted view of freedom in which the role of the public is essential. These issues are not only of interest for discussions within the capabilities approach. Broadly speaking, the argument is that a socially constituted view of agency does not have to lead to pessimistic conclusions regarding freedom of action. Dewey's theory of the public also lends credence to the idea that capabilities are a public issue. Next I will, again, go through some related issues in more detail.

Capabilities, Values and Freedom

Sen's starting point is the assertion that poverty is traditionally seen as an economic phenomenon, irrespective of whether it is defined in absolute or relative terms. However, poverty can also be seen as "a deprivation of basic capabilities, rather than merely low income" (Sen 2001, 20). Capabilities refer to various combinations of functionings that relate to things that we value and have reason to do so. Deprivation of capabilities can manifest itself, for example, in premature mortality and widespread illiteracy. There are many reasons for assessing the distribution of income within a population but analysis should not end here. Sen (ibid., 21) presents disturbing evidence that deprivation can be even greater for some groups in the quite well-off Western countries than for those living in developing countries. For example, African Americans in the United States have lower chances of living long lives than people in China or in the state of Kerala in India. This finding is in line with Sen's general argument because African Americans are by far richer than people in China or Kerala. Thus, economic prosperity does not automatically indicate that people lead longer lives. Therefore an income-centered view of poverty can be misleading in many cases.

Sen is not opposed to markets as such even though he is a critic of economism as a social philosophy. He argues that if people are denied access to market transactions, this can be a form of unfreedom in itself. If one looks at the history of Western societies, it is undeniable that the transition from forms of bonded labor to labor markets with free contracts advanced freedom. And, as Sen (2001, 28) reminds us, bonded labor is still a reality in many economies of the world. When development is seen as freedom one is not obliged to demonstrate that labor markets raise productivity – their effect on the advancement of freedom should be enough in this perspective. Unlike many economists, who vote for some sort of individualism as a political stance, Sen argues that freedom is a result of the social environment. One can also suggest that freedom has a double role: it is both the end and the means of development.

Sen's position is in many ways close to the ideas of pragmatism, although pragmatism does not play a role in his writings. For example, in his latest book Sen (2010) tries to ground the search for the idea of justice in existing inequalities rather than in utopian and transcendental institutional arrangements (as in Rawlsian political thought). This grounding is thus very pragmatic provides yet another reason for discussing Sen in relation to pragmatism. However, I am not trying to cover up the differences between these theoretical approaches. The main dissimilarity probably has to do with the fact that Sen forcefully emphasizes the ability to choose things whereas pragmatism mainly sees things in terms of habits. For example, Sen (ibid., 227) argues that we have reason to be interested "in the freedom that we have actually to choose between different styles and ways of living." One could, however, wonder whether there are actual choices involved in matters having to do with lifestyles. Sen seems to think that we do not ponder upon every decision we make due to habit-formation but this formation of habits only happens after "the reasons for a particular choice are established in our mind" (ibid., 181). Again, one might argue that in many cases no explicit reasons are there to begin with. However, pragmatists – Dewey in particular – have also cultivated an attitude of reflexive habituality. This is an attitude which does not attempt to do away with habits but rather tries to reflect on their consequences for us and the world. Thus, there are no insurmountable differences in this regard between Sen and pragmatism.

Sen wants to reserve an active role for people – as objects of developmental reforms and in general. He does this by referring to the values that people have and to public discussion which can influence the values that we have. However, as I argue, referring to values can run the risk of positing them as yet another prime mover of action – values as ultimate ends of action, for example. Thorstein Veblen (2002) has called the postulate that some prime movers of action always exist the utilitarian fallacy. As discussed in the context of institution theories, Veblen was influenced by pragmatist naturalism, which led him to conclude that humans always are in action, and therefore motives are part of ongoing action processes. Motives naturally play a role in action but this role is confined to situations where the normal course of action, habitual action, is blocked for some reason or another and a crisis of action is imminent. Then the actor has to ponder on his or her motives and the available means and ends, these latter two always being intertwined (Whitford 2002). This pondering can often include value judgments but strictly speaking these judgments are not necessarily always present even in these sorts of crises. Furthermore, there are also cases when people can say that they have all sorts of values but in the end they act according to their habits (for example, in relation to environmental issues). However, one could argue that public discussion can act as an initiator of crises, which forces people to reflect on their habits.

My main discussion of Sen relates to the issue of freedom being a product of social conditions. If freedom is indeed a social product, does it not indicate that we have to give in to such relativist views which downplay its significance? Sen discusses this issue by referring to discussions on so-called Asian values. It has been suggested that Asian values are authoritarian and therefore they are very different from Western values. However, this argument has usually been employed by leaders of non-democratic countries who want to justify their own position of power. Western thinkers have not always fared any better owing to a tendency to assume that political freedom and democracy have somehow always been features of Western culture. This argumentative tendency exhibits an extrapolation backwards from the present situation (Sen 2001, 233). In other words, issues of freedom are in reality children of the Enlightenment and other quite recent historical events. One can find both authoritarian features in the history of the West and the highlighting of the value of freedom in Asia. From this finding Sen concludes that capabilities – and also public reasoning and democracy (Sen 2010, Ch. 15) – should be of interest in all cultural milieus. However, my argument is that freedom (and thus also capabilities) are an issue that arises as a consequence of human self-reflexivity and therefore discussing these issues is not an ethnocentric agenda. Nussbaum argues along similar lines when she proposes that "[w]hen we speak simply of what people are actually able to do and to be, we do not even give the appearance of privileging a Western idea" (Nussbaum 2000, 100).

Introduction: Grounds for Pragmatism

Freedom has, according to Sen (2001, 246), intrinsic importance but in addition it has two important roles: a consequential and a constructive role. The first role has to do with the fact that political freedom can prevent economic catastrophes, such as famines, because the incentives for their prevention are in place only when political leaders are accountable to the public. Thus, no widespread famines have occurred in democratic countries. The constructive role of freedom is related to free speech as a generator of values and new cultural priorities. One might argue that freedom promotes "social construction" but this does not mean that freedom is merely arbitrary construction. Problems relating to capabilities are in essence *moral* problems and they come about especially in conflicting situations. The value of these circumstances is in a reconstruction of the situation that calls for reflexive evaluation where one can see "the development of a self more inclusive in its social concerns and interests than was the self for whom the problem initially arose," as Mead scholar Gary A. Cook (1993, 121) puts it.

I have already discussed Mead at length but it is time to bring him into the discussion once more. If freedom is a social product then Mead's conception of intersubjectivity as a precondition for reflexivity is important. Reflexivity allows one to focus on the relationship between the organism and its environment. In the case of humans, this has led to the environment being to a large extent cultural. Mere adaptation to different environments is therefore not the only option because environments can also be actively constructed by as cultural "niches" (cf. Sterelny 2003). From these premises it follows that social control is essentially about *self-criticism*:

> The general social process of experience and behaviour which the group is carrying on is directly presented to him in his own experience, and so that he is thereby able to govern and direct his conduct consciously and critically, with reference to his relations both to the social group as a whole and to its other individual members, in terms of this social process. Thus he becomes not only self-conscious but also self-critical; and thus, through self-criticism, social control over individual behavior or conduct operates by virtue of the social origin and basis of such criticism. (Mead 1967, 255.)

So far even an everyday critical theorist might agree but things get more complicated when we come to Mead's conclusion: "Hence social control, so far from tending to crush out the human individual or to obliterate his self-conscious individuality, is, on the contrary, actually constitutive of and inextricably associated with that of individuality" (ibid.). Of course, one can think of situations where social control actually crushes individuality but this sort of repression is not a general feature of social control in the Meadian sense. Thus, if intersubjectivity is a precondition for self-reflexivity then freedom is indeed a social product.

The Public and the Publics

The second part of the discussion concerns the issue of how should the relevant capabilities be decided if Sen does not want to present us with a list of what they should be. As mentioned above, Sen's general idea is that these issues should be discussed publicly because important social values can emerge as a result. These arguments seem forceful. Thus, I present Dewey's theory of the public as a support rather than as a challenge to them. The background of Dewey's account of the public is in a debate with Walter Lippmann (Westbrook 1991, 293-318; Whipple 2005), a major representative of so-called democratic realism in the 1920s. For Lippmann, citizens in a modern society are so uninformed that the unavoidable conclusion is that most decision-making should be left to insiders with the required expert knowledge. Dewey shared Lippmann's concerns about the state of democracy but he did not endorse Lippmann's elitist agenda. Rather, Dewey paid special attention to the difference that proper education and a real democratic culture can make in people's lives. In addition, Dewey thought that democracy is inherent in the idea of community life itself because democracy refers to being aware of such life, in "all its implications" (Dewey 1927, 149). Thus, there really are no proper alternatives to democracy. The role of the public in voicing social problems is essential in fostering democratic self-awareness and self-governance.

What is problematic for Dewey is that the birth of a "Great Society" with its uprooting effects has not coincided with the coming about of a "Great Community." Modernization has been liberating to individual people because it has released "human potentialities previously dormant," but the same liberating factors were unsettling to many communities (Dewey 1927, 98-99). These factors were also damaging to the idea of the public because both the community and the public entail that the consequences of associated activity are perceived (ibid., 151). In a Great Society these consequences are harder to perceive than before due to their complex and far-reaching nature. This situation still calls for communicative activity with shared signs and symbols (ibid., 153).

One should not forget that Dewey did not rely on "mere" discussion as a vehicle of politics. Discussion is indispensable for the elaboration of ideas but it is not the sole source of "systematic origination of comprehensive plans" (Dewey 2000, 73). A heavy reliance of politics on discussion is also reflected in a conception which treats intelligence as an individualistic possession. In Dewey's opinion, blind trust in mere discussion and the notion of individualistic intelligence are to be replaced with social intelligence which is exemplified by scientific inquiry. To some skeptics this glorifying of scientific procedures can sound like positivism or even scientism. However, the scientific method can be defined so that it embodies a form of social intelligence and is therefore a complementary practice with an emphasis on the public. Deweyan social inquiry is the antithesis of relying on individual prejudices or on mere habits of opinion because inquiry calls for testing by consequences (Dewey 2000, 40). One should also remember that what Dewey was arguing for in the 1920s is to some extent a reality today: political decision-making utilizes information provided by research institutes, for example. These research institutes, however, tend to take their objectives as given and tend to provide crumbs of information instead of the aforementioned "systematic origination of comprehensive plans." They are also often in danger of losing sight of the importance of our embodied and habitual interactions as sources of rationalities of action because they often rely on quite intellectualistic views of action (on rational choice theory, for example).

In the original article I argue that capabilities are subject to important social issues, and also that their effect on these issues is so vast that they are clearly in need of public regulation. First, what they need is protection from structural influences. For example, economic recessions undoubtedly affect the capabilities of large numbers of people, and therefore adequate unemployment benefits and other safety measures are needed. This is not enough, however, because also active promotion of capabilities is also important due to the significant effects of capabilities on economic development (among other things). Social change can raise economic productivity but its effect on the advancement of freedom is what really counts.

It is then the role of the public to articulate problems that lead to the disruption of social habits. "Without an adequate public to help us, individuals cannot understand the meaning of the constant stream of events and its attendant information," as Campbell (1998, 37) interprets Dewey. Jürgen Habermas famously highlights the importance of rational debate on a consensus-level, whereas Dewey explicates the formation of publics on the bases of problematic situations. These situations call for the reconstruction of the social "order," but they also reconstruct selves or personalities because the relationship between social and personality reconstruction is more or less reciprocal (Mead 1967, 309). The role of the public is then to watch over democracy so that issues affecting third parties get duly noticed and officials keep their own interest in check.

In a so-called realist vision of politics (the view held by Lippmann), democracy is about citizens choosing representatives for themselves every few years. This is also a chance *not* to elect those representatives that have been too keen on advancing their own interest. For realists, the ultimate scenario to be feared is one of ignorant masses having too much say in the business of government. Therefore governing should be left to experts and elites and the public's participation is required only for purposes of legitimation. The problem with this view is that no one is there to guard the public against the possible attempts by governing elites to manipulate public opinion, "thereby negating the power of public desires and interests to act as independent variables in policy making" (Westbrook 1991, 544). In the realist view, there is a strict dichotomy between the private and the public, where the former is a place for self-fulfillment. This stance is in clear contradiction with Dewey's and Mead's arguments; both thinkers argued that participation in the matters of community life is a prerequisite for self-fulfillment because the self is born in a social process in the first place; consequently the self never completely unties the strings attaching it to its social environment.

As mentioned, Sen fundamentally presents a very market-friendly picture of social reconstruction. This can be seen, for example, in his assessment that labor markets are basically a good thing because they free people from bonded labor relations. Probably no one in their right minds would argue that bonded relations are desirable, but one can disagree as to how free labor markets are in reality. Karl Marx erred in many ways but he made an important observation when he argued that the labor contract is never really free because it is never made between equal partners. Labor unions have been the Social Democratic answer to this problem, and Sen probably would not disagree as to their merits. However, one can ask the very fundamental question whether a market-oriented society is compatible with democracy. Some might argue that there really is nothing as democratic as market-oriented steering mechanisms because they tell us what people want, not what bureaucrats or politicians think people want. However, it is well known that the one-dollar-one-vote system would be democratic only if everyone had the same amount of dollars at their disposal. This clearly is not the case in any existing democracy.

Furthermore, one can ponder whether it is reasonable to see labor as a commodity in the first place. Karl Polanyi (2001) argued famously that labor is a *fictive commodity*. It is not originally a "product" for markets because it consists of human labor which exists already before any markets are put into place. Humans are always in action, as pragmatists would argue. The channels that action takes can, of course, be directed with different incentives but it is a fiction to think of labor as a commodity like any other. What can make this fictive notion even harmful is that it can prevent one from seeing its nature as human action. Therefore too much market-friendliness – seeing everything as commodities – can produce a situation where individuals are seen as passive creatures and mere producers of commodity-labor.

Even though Dewey was not a socialist in any dogmatic sense, he still thought that capitalism inhibits the formation of participatory democracy which was essential to his vision of democracy as a key to self-development and social reconstruction (Westbrook 1991, 434). Dewey's vision leaned on the bedrock of reforming educational institutions but it also demanded (in a fashion somewhat akin to Marxism) that the means of production should not be in the hands of the few (e.g., Dewey 2000, 67-68). He also argued that applying the scientific method to social issues "has been conditioned by the system to which the name of capitalism is given," capitalism meaning "a rough designation of a complex of political and legal arrangements centering about a particular mode of economic relations" (ibid., 77). However, Dewey was not placing his bets on class struggle as a method of social change. This move was not an attempt to deny the existence of conflicting interests but rather an effort to highlight the essence of democracy as a way to openly discuss these interests and to balance them with a larger social perspective in mind (ibid., 81). Conflicts then call for the method of the Meadian attitude of the generalized other, which means generalizing from particular perspectives. However, capitalism tends to favor a view of actors as autonomous and separate and this can be contradictory to generalizing from particular perspectives.

This is not to say that Dewey's vision of the public is without its own problems. One major theme that is undertheorized in his work relates to the issue of *how* and *why* the public emerges. One occasionally gets the impression that it is almost like an automatic process: when there are important problems affecting so-called third parties, then it just emerges. When one looks at historical cases in retrospect, it can seem that the public was indeed bound to emerge. For example, the fall of the Soviet empire and related revolutions often feel as if they were just waiting to happen (due to the inherent problems of the Soviet system). However, such superficial analyses mask the fact that there always has to be an active *social movement* to articulate concerns and grievances. This process presupposes a politicization of the issue(s) in question; that is, the process of naming and articulating something as political (Luhtakallio 2010). Thus, Dewey himself is not so concerned with the practicalities and with the actual agents of this process and for this reason should not be relied upon as the only source in research on the public.

MacGilvaray (2010) has drawn attention to the fact that Dewey also tends to think of public issues in terms of *the* public. Thus, in Dewey's vision, there should be one public which represents the interests of all parties concerned. This might be too much to ask nationally – and even more so in a global perspective. It is not surprising that in recent times it has become more popular to speak of the public in the plural. However, one might still argue that some sorts of forums for the meeting of different perspectives are necessarily called for. Such forums can then be called "the public." For example, Bohman (2010, 53) has argued that "the diversity of perspective is what provides the epistemic benefits of deliberation by publics which makes possible the recognition that there are common interests." Thus, although there probably should be a "transformation from a unitary to a disaggregated or distributive form" (ibid., 63), this does not necessarily imply that there is no common ground to be found. However, this issue is not only that the public should recognize itself but also one of representing the interests of those affected by the problems at hand.

A second problematic issue has to do with Dewey's seemingly communitarian bent. The importance of the community can seem too vast in his scheme. It is, after all, a moral idea. Furthermore, "there is not just the danger of too little community, but that of too much as well," as Beck and Beck-Gernsheim (2002, 166) argue. The public should surely be able to have a sense of being "metatopical" (cf. Taylor

2004, ch. 6). However, as in the case of Mead's thought, Dewey's communitarianism is not of the traditional variety. In Deweyan (and Meadian) communitarianism, sociality does not crush individuality and is not restricted to particular "topics." Dewey's argument is that "individuals grow to a sense of self-consciousness *through* the communities in which they live, not simply *in* them" (Campbell 1998, 24). This process enables a critical attitude towards one's communities. One can also argue that the "demand for freedom from conventions, from given laws (…) is only possible where the individual appeals, so to speak, from a narrow and restricted community to a larger one" (Mead 1967, 199). Individual self-reflection also takes place by not relying on some purely individual perspective but by looking at things from a larger perspective; through generalized, shared responses. Thus, a narrow parochialism can be avoided by taking this larger perspective into account.

CHAPTER 2

The Over- or the Undersocialized Conception of Man? Practice Theory and the Problem of Intersubjectivity[21]

"If our assumptions are left implicit, we will inevitably presuppose a view of man that is tailor-made to our special needs; when our sociological theory over-stresses the stability and integration of society we will end up imagining that man is the disembodied, conscience-driven, status-seeking phantom of current theory." Thus Dennis H. Wrong (1961, 193) formulated his famous critique of Parsonian sociology. The latter leads, according to Wrong, to an oversocialized view of man, because Parsonian norm-internalization excluded the inner conflicts and tensions that Freudian psychology captured. Today norms and their internalization are no longer the paradigmatic question in sociology. However, the same kinds of problems of oversocialization still plague the discipline, as Wrong (1999) himself has noticed in a later writing. There he admits that his classical paper "by no means succeeded in eliminating oversocialized conceptions of human nature from social theory." Present-day theory claims that "just about every human activity is the product of 'social construction.'" (Ibid., x.) The problem with social constructionism is that it tends to emphasize the role of knowledge and language at the expense of other important issues. It is no accident that Peter Berger and Thomas Luckmann's famous book *The Social Construction of Reality* (1966) had a subtitle which declared it to be *A Treatise in the Sociology of Knowledge*. There is nothing wrong with concentrating on the analysis of knowledge as such, but problems are bound to arise when knowledge is treated as the only possible realm of meaning. If and when this is done, then the realm of the *"social"* tends to attract more than its due share in explaining, e.g., action. The immense interest in discursive factors in social analysis testifies to this state of affairs.

---

21 This chapter was originally published in *Sociology* (2008), 42:2, 243-259.

The most challenging and fruitful critiques of social constructionism have come from the protagonists of practice theory. Some practice theorists are close to constructionism and "culturalism" and therefore they try to incorporate the insights of constructionism into practice theory (e.g., Reckwitz 2002). The most interesting discussions in practice theory, however, do not claim that practices are the products of social construction. In this article I discuss one such attempt, the realist practice theory of Margaret Archer. I am using her theory to highlight the main fault of constructionism, namely, the over-emphasis on social discourses. I also argue that Archer goes too far with her critiques so that the result is *an undersocialized* picture of selfhood and agency. This result can be seen in her dismissal of George Herbert Mead's pragmatist theory of selfhood, which is the reason why I have concentrated on analyzing how Mead should be understood if we want to use his work in critiques of constructionism – and as a constructive theory of action. These are certainly plausible and productive ways of "operationalizing" Mead. It is my intention, then, to focus critically on practice theory and especially on the issue and role of sociality within practice theory.

Margaret Archer has been at the forefront of Anglo-American social theory at least since the publication of her *Culture and Agency* (1988). She is well-known for her criticism of Anthony Giddens' structuration theory. Archer takes for granted neither methodological individualism nor holism because she opposes the duality of action and structure – action and structure as part of the same process. She maintains that they have to be analytically separated from each other because structures antecede action as constraining and enabling factors. According to her, structures are ontologically real emergent properties of action (for debates of Archer's ideas, see, for example, Vandenberghe 2005; Hodgson 2004; Mutch 2004; Sawyer 2001; Stones 2001; Schilling 1999; Zeuner 1999). In sociology Archer is also famous as a spokesperson for critical realism, which is elsewhere associated with the names of Roy Bhaskar and Andrew Sayer.

However, in this article the main focus is not on the debate between critical realists and their Giddensian opponents. In her book, *Structure, Agency and the Internal Conversation* (2003), Archer is critical of various forms of sociological reductionism that fuse conceptions of selfhood and selves. The case in point is a special instance of the so-called epistemological fallacy, i.e., treating concepts as if they were the very things that they refer to. This fallacy has been at play in some forms of social constructionism in sociology. As mentioned, Archer's remedy to this reductionist tendency is to emphasize the role of practice and the pre-social nature of selfhood. Her diagnosis is certainly correct in that social theory and sociology need more emphasis on practice and action instead of mere knowledge and conceptual analysis. Yet Archer makes some wrong moves on her way, which weaken the very foundations of her project. First of all, we end up with an undersocialized view of selfhood, as I have already indicated. A second problem has to do with the interest of practice theory in the relationship between action and social structures. Archer's theory is no exception; it reminds us that actors can take reflexive stances toward structures. However, her theory tends to downplay the role of habitual dispositions in maintaining structures, which gives me a reason to argue for the importance of habits. These particular issues are not only of interest for Archer scholars – or for Mead scholars – but also for the general sociological public. It is my purpose to discuss these particular authors in a manner that highlights some of the most important questions of sociology and social theory in general.

Practice and Sociality

Critiques of rational choice theories have been quite common in sociology in recent years (e.g., Archer & Tritter 2000). Such criticisms have been important reminders that action is not only about calculative operations of selecting among alternative options. However, a second set of issues that relates to issues of action theory, the role of discursive factors, has not received due attention in critical discussions. There is, of course, Hacking's (1999) analysis of different strands of social constructionism and Campbell's (1995) attempt to rescue theories of action from the hands of "social situationalists." Perhaps the most well-known effort of trying to frame discursive phenomena in a broader context can be observed, however, in practice theory. Schatzki et al. (2001) have gone so far as to discuss *The Practice turn in Contemporary Theory* (as the title of their book claims). Archer's argumentation belongs to this latter tradition.

Central to realist thinking in practice theory is the presupposition that "our sense of self, as part of humanity, is prior and primitive to our sociality" (Archer 2000, 121). Without this postulate the self will be absorbed by sociality, and at the same time it will be deprived of its autonomy and its causal efficacy. In order to avoid this state of affairs, it can be claimed that in addition to intentional causal action we share bodily self-consciousness with other higher animal species, which means that these capabilities are not social "gifts." The self, which is the "continuous sense of being the one and the same subject, emerges *early in life* and is the source of reflexive self-consciousness" (ibid., 255). Archer objects to two opposing views, which either tend to reduce humanity to rational choice or to social influences. In the first option, man is a rational chooser whose constitution is not in any way related to society, whereas the second option leads one to think of human constitution (e.g., selfhood) as deriving exclusively from discursive factors. Both conceptions are guilty of reductionism, even though this reduction is performed in opposite directions.

We have to engage in practical work in the world the moment we are born, and this practice is not dependent on social influences. Instead, it depends on "a learning process through which the continuous sense of self emerges" (ibid., 122). Practical action requires the actor to be capable of separating him- or herself from the world. This capability or "sense" is independent of its linguistic encoding, which means that it is not the product of linguistic or social construction. Concepts discussing the self are indeed social but "the universal sense of self" is not social because it is "naturally grounded" (ibid., 124). This argument suggests that the social is somehow opposed to or at least different from the natural realm. It also tends to equate sociality with concepts or with language in general, which is not appropriate.

However, it is important to warn about the dangers of absorbing "the sense into the *concept*," of which some versions of constructionism are guilty of (Archer 2002, 12). And this is exactly why practice needs a primary place in social theory. The importance of non-social practice aligns practice theory close to Husserlian phenomenology with the essential difference that epistemology should not have priority over ontology as in Husserl's thinking. Archer writes that

> The human body is unique, because of its dual role as the source of perception which is also able to sense itself. It is particularly in touching oneself, where there is only one sensation, unlike touching a table when toucher and touched are distinct, that the self-consciousness which constitutes me as a subject, rather than object, arises. (Archer 2000, 130.)

Thus Archer postulates that self-consciousness arises out of mere contact experiences with the world and in particular with oneself. It is undeniably true that humans and animals – higher and "lower" ones included – share intentionality as the ability for "aboutness," i.e., the ability to navigate or to act purposefully in the world (and to touch oneself if need be). But to have this ability does not necessarily mean that one is aware or conscious of having it. To act intentionally, then, does not always mean that there is a self who knows what it is doing or that there is awareness of that self. To have this awareness – and even us humans do not have it all the time – is not the same thing as a proper consciousness of the self. It might be that there is a sense of self-awareness of the body that even some animals are capable of but this is not the same thing as having "self-consciousness in the sense that they [i.e., animals] can reflect on their being conscious" (Gärdenfors 2003, 14, 119).

Nevertheless, language enables causal effects of "mind upon mind," so that we can, for example, elicit sympathy by using expressive language (Archer 2000, 158). Practice also leads to knowledge that is non-linguistic in character. Archer claims that Anthony Giddens regards practical knowledge as being structured *like* language. This is not so, Archer maintains, and I agree, but something is still missing here. Why use the word knowledge about practical ways of "knowing" in the first place if we are mainly discussing habitual dispositions? This only leads one to use residual categories such as "tacit knowledge" or "bodily knowledge" (cf. Bourdieu 2000). If we want a separate word for it, then why not use "information" instead of "knowledge" which should be reserved for discursive phenomena. It follows that a shared characteristic between humans and animals is not "embodied knowledge" because this sort of information is not knowledge. Of course, it can be claimed that embodied knowledge is "real knowledge" because its misuse is regulative: "There is an incorrect way of doing things which indicates that there are such things as embodied rules" (Archer 2000, 164). Two wrongs do not make a right, however. The concept of a rule is useful in many ways, but it is an intellectualistic strategy to use it to describe *all* action that manifests uniform features. At the bodily level, which can be called the pre-reflective level of meaning, no rules, strictly speaking, appear at all because no one is (knowingly) following a rule (Heiskala 2003, 269).[22] I will deal with this question more thoroughly in the last section of my paper where I discuss the role of habits.

According to practice theory, we acquire a personal identity, a self, just by acting in the world. Social identity in the form of social expectations is appropriated by actors, but for this to happen there already has to be a sense of self that can recognize these expectations and act accordingly (Archer 2000, 256). Social identity, then, is assumed in society, whereas personal identity "regulates the subject's relations with reality as a whole" (ibid., 257). This means that a personal identity and a self are already in place before any social identities can be appropriated. All of this is in line with a stratified conception of reality where reality is divided into different realms (personal, social, etc.). However, it is problematic to view the self as a static personal identity, as something that is born once and then regulates the subject's relations with social reality. One can also wonder whether human subjects ever really confront reality outside of society. Apparently not, because the world we act in and our reactions to it are social in the first place. Of course, one can go hiking by oneself into the wilderness, but even there one never quite leaves one's "society" behind in the sense that one usually relates one's environment to social attitudes (reflexes precluded, e.g., dodging a falling rock).

Here one should be very careful whether to affirm the old sociological conception whereby actors are seen as social only when other actors are present, because there is a big difference between being gregarious and being social, as Charles Peirce (CP 1.11)[23] pointed out. Gregarious animals react to different stimuli coming from members of their own species and they are able to co-operate with each other, at least in a rudimentary manner. But this does not mean that they are properly speaking social in the sense that they would be aware of social stimuli or that they would "take the roles of the other." Having said all of this, one can still reserve a place for private and subjective meanings. This place is found in internal conversations.

22 The concept of rule is used by Archer in a manner that implies that rules are really ontologically present at this pre-reflective level, which is a problematic suggestion. See Turner (2002).
23 This is the traditional way of referring to Peirce's Collected Papers in which CP is an abbreviation of the title; in this instance, 1 refers to the number of the volume and 11 to the paragraph in question.

Exit Introspection, Enter Reflexivity

Archer's focus on internal conversations is an attempt to rescue the private realm of the mind from the hands of those constructionists who see the mind as nothing else but socially inscribed meanings. In contrast with these constructionist attempts, we have the traditional model of introspection. It is based on the presumption that there is a special sense or a sense organ that functions as a vehicle for the inspection of inner conscious states (Archer 2003, 21). Normal perception is based on "a clear distinction between the object we see and our visual experiences of it, whereas with introspection there can be no such differentiation between the object and the spectator, since I am supposedly looking inward at myself" (ibid.). Archer objects to there being such a special inner sense. The private life of the mind, however, is in need of rescue from the reductions of behaviorists and culturalists alike. This private life is none other than reflexivity itself in which "the subject deliberates upon how some item, such as belief, desire, idea or state of affairs pertains or relates to itself" (ibid., 26).

Archer's argument is not the first time this idea has been brought out in social theory. For example, during the heyday of pragmatism it was discussed at length. As Archer develops her version of the internal conversation, pragmatism's founder Charles Peirce is a hero, whereas a fellow pragmatist, G. H. Mead, is Archer's villain. Peirce maintained that thought is dialogical and in it the inner world of the subject is realized through the use of intersubjective signs. The public media are, however, always used privately and innovatively. (Ibid., 66-70.) At first glance one might think that practice theorists would rejoice in the fact that as a pragmatist, Mead insists on the relevance of action in a manner that resembles practice theory. Mead supposedly claimed that when conversing with oneself, one is actually conversing with society. According to Archer (ibid., 79), "the 'Me' is really the 'We' – what Mead called the 'generalised other'", i.e., nothing else but a product of social construction. It is certainly correct to assign to Mead the idea that one can become an object to oneself only by taking the attitudes of others toward oneself. Thus, one can become reflexive and self-conscious only when one has developed a self, and its development is a social process. This is presumably in contradiction to practice thinkers for whom the self as an object emerges through mere natural and practical relations. But what did Mead actually argue? I am not intending to write a thorough Mead exegesis, but it is worthwhile to pause and consider Mead's theory, because it has something unique to offer for the debate on the role of sociality in the "private realm."

First of all, we have to remember that Mead's thinking was born of the pragmatist tradition, and this means that we derive the most from his thinking if we approach his theory from this perspective (cf. Joas 1985). Properly speaking, Mead was neither a sociologist nor a social psychologist; his main interests were meta-sociological, i.e., they had to do with the prerequisites of sociality. In addition, it is a mistake to consider him as being interested only in the formation of selfhood. Pragmatism's main idea is the so-called doubt-belief theory of inquiry (Kilpinen 2000), which argues that reflection is made possible by the inhibition of action for one reason or another (Mead 1967, 90-1). In such cases, the possibility opens up for the human actor to reflect on his or her possible responses before actually responding. In order to reflect, one must have a "mind," i.e., an inner representation of reality (cf. Gärdenfors 2003). However, Mead does not want to place the mind inside a brain or even inside an individual because of his pragmatist leitmotif of action. The mind is a process that "lies in a field of conduct between a specific individual and the environment, in which the individual is able, through the generalized attitude he assumes, to make use of symbolic gestures, i.e., terms, which are significant to all including himself" (Mead 1922, 247).

A great deal does indeed depend on the environment of the organism (generally speaking). Every organism is always acting within a certain environment, and this means that the "organization of the self is simply the organization, by the individual organism, of the set of attitudes toward its social environment – and toward itself from the standpoint of that environment" (Mead 1967, 91). However, the environment is also dependent on the organism. For example, "grass" is distinguished from its environment as an object only by those animals that use it for nourishment. What gets picked out from the environment, then, are those stimuli that somehow relate to the organisms' action process. This interrelationship between action processes and stimuli does not make those objects subjective because "the natures of the objects are in the objects" (Mead 1922, 241).[24] Pragmatism is not then a straightforward denial of the distinction between epistemology and ontology that realist practice theory cherishes. However, one might call the pragmatist position transactional as it is both the agent and the environment that have a say in the action process (cf. Khalil 2004). Or to formulate this important point in another manner, the "stimulus and response reciprocally affect one another" (Cook 2006, 70).

For practice theory, consciousness of a self develops through practical action in the world; even animals have this capacity for bodily self-consciousness. According to Mead (1967, 94), what differentiates the human organism from "lower" animals is the capacity for rational conduct, which consists of indications where one points out to oneself or to others the proper stimuli in a certain situation: "[by] holding on to the stimulus we can get control of the response." Strictly speaking, self-consciousness then necessitates this ability to *understand* the possible stimuli and responses in a given situation, and this is precisely what is lacking in animals. Of course, animals react to proper stimuli (e.g., to grass as nourishment and to other members of their species), and their responses can be affected via conditioning, but they do not understand that they are responding in a certain manner – there is no self that would be capable of assessing the stimuli in relation to itself.

24 What makes an object subjective is its "being referred by an individual to his self" (Mead 1922, 242).

So far, so good for rational, reflexive conduct, which is "the essential condition (…) for the development of mind" (Mead 1967, 134).[25] What, then, is the relationship of mind to self-consciousness? As the term implies, for there to be self-consciousness, there needs to be a self. Animals do not have a self since they only have a body that nevertheless enables more or less proper – but quite rigid – conduct in a given environment. Animals might be able to have the sort of bodily consciousness that Archer claims but this does not mean that they are conscious of *themselves*. A self is by definition characterized by self-referentiality because it is an object to itself – or more precisely, it can be both a subject and an object. The reason for this development is probably evolutionary, since being an object to oneself enhances the ability to adapt to different environments with ease: "without taking objective account of itself (…) it [the actor] cannot act intelligently, or rationally" (ibid., 138). With a self one can, so to speak, take the attitude of the environment toward oneself.

The developmental way of becoming an object to oneself, i.e., of being self-conscious, is through taking the attitudes of other actors within a certain social environment. An attitude is a mental disposition, but it has very concrete consequences because it is a "tendency to respond in a certain manner to certain sorts of stimuli" (Cook 1993, 79). Taking the attitudes or the roles of others means that one anticipates their responses to our action (Aboulafia 2006, 198). As mentioned earlier, Archer lumps Mead together with the constructionists of our day, and in this she is clearly wrong. Nonetheless, there is a grain of truth in her claim. Unlike some "naïve" realists of his time, Mead (1925, 271) was not content with assigning "all the qualities of things to the things, over against a mind which was simply aware of the sensa [i.e., sensations]." This assignment would lead to a hopeless "psycho-physical parallelism" where we have objects and their qualities and a consciousness that is somehow aware of these things. Mead's displeasure with this line of thinking is due to the fact that objects are always in a relation to ongoing conduct: "The percept is relative to the perceiving individual, but relative to his active interest, not relative in the sense that its content is a state of his consciousness" (ibid., 270). This is not naïve realism, but neither is it idealism in any of its usual forms.

If the self is understood as taking the attitude of others, then it is not only a contemplative exercise because it arises in conduct, as does basically anything worthy of the sociologist's attention. The self emerges through the use of a gesture "which another individual would use and [one] responds to it himself, or tends so to respond" (Mead 1922, 243). When this happens, the *meaning* of the gesture is understood, and this understanding is by definition shared. In this case it is justified to talk of signif-

---

25 Rationality so conceived does not necessarily imply a calculating attitude toward the stimuli, and it most certainly does not mean that actors would always act in such a stimuli-analyzing manner in the first place. I will elaborate on this later with the concept of habit.

icant symbols. The prime example is the vocal gesture, i.e., language. This argument should also illuminate the assertion that the mind is not confined to the individual or to the brain because significance is a relation between things and individuals.

As it happens, modern cognitive science has dealt with the issue of how self-consciousness emerges in a developing human being. According to Bogdan (2003, 89), who reviews many studies on the subject, reflexivity consists of "metarepresentations" that represent thoughts as a mental relation to certain content: "one categorizes a thought as a thought (explicitly represents its mental identity) *and* specifies its content in terms of other thoughts." This reflexive capacity to mind your own mind is, however, dependent on the ability to mind other minds. One interprets one's own mind because one takes the perspective of others on one's self. When one re-represents from the "inside but in socially relational terms, the self becomes a *reflexive self*, a self that looks at its mental exploits *as* others would, from their (interpretative) perspectives" (ibid., 173). Here we have the fully intersubjective self that Mead pictured in his work long before cognitive science was born as a discipline – in contrast to a merely interactive being that only sees bodily movements and is not capable of imagining any minds, those of others, or that of its own (see also Baron-Cohen 1995). Thus, we can say that Mead's pragmatist philosophy prefigured the empirical results of cognitive science.

The concept of the generalized other is somewhat imprecise, and this is bound to lead to confusion. However, contrary to what Archer and some others claim (e.g., Wiley 1994, 47), there is nothing psychologically repressive in the conception of the generalized other. Without a generalized other there would be no intelligent thought – private or public – because meaning proper entails *a generalized attitude* that indicates it to both the self and to others as well (Mead 1922, 247). In other words, the concept refers to the general social process and does not say anything about its particular contents, which certainly can, in many cases, be repressive. However, there is always the creative output of the individual "I" that reacts to the habitual and conservative "me." In Mead's pragmatism we find a possibility for autonomy that is "no longer an original given that is to be opposed to society" (Joas 1985, 35).

There are as many relevant attitudes of others as there are relevant social circles in one's action process at a given time, and these are always unique to the self in question. And what is even more important: "we are not only what is common to all: each one of the selves is different from everyone else" (Mead 1967, 163). A "multiple personality" – in the sense of taking the attitudes of many others – is not unusual, but the different attitudes of others are still normally unified within the self. This unity is the generalized other, and it in fact is what enables thinking, as I already indicated (cf. Sacks 1995). If the different attitudes are not unified, then a crisis of action is imminent and it is probably the result of problems in the unity of the whole social process of the actor in question. There are many occasions when the actor and its environment are not in perfect "equilibrium," but "the self goes to pieces," as John Dewey (2002, 179) remarks, only when there is a "complete crushing of organized activity."

Furthermore, these others are not necessarily people one personally knows, but rather certain thought currents that one finds attractive. For example, I could be a committed practice theorist even if I had never met any practice theorists personally. As the reader might have guessed by now, I am not really a committed practice theorist, but some of the ideas of practice theory I nevertheless find useful. This brings us to the conclusion that there can be competing attitudes that one takes on; I am more of a committed pragmatist than anything else in my action process at the moment, and this is the light in which I "take the attitude of practice theory" and evaluate its ideas. Of course, I can be mistaken in my evocation of this line of thinking, and this means that taking on the attitudes of others is subject to fallibility – as is human action in general. What the Meadian/pragmatist perspective brings to our attention is that one is usually social, not only when explicitly interacting with other people but also in solitary situations. Animals can interact, but they are not social in the intersubjective sense even if they are in the company of other members of their species.

Internal Conversation, Social Structures, and Habitual Action

So far I have tried to find a niche for the private realm from the imperialistic tendencies of social constructionism. But what should we actually place within this sphere? Again, Archer has a useful line of argumentation. It is an attempt to answer three interrelated questions: first, "how can the self be both subject and object at the same time;" second, if thought consists of internal dialogue, then "who is speaking to whom;" and third, "if our reflections do concern society (...), [then] how does the societal get into the conversational process" (Archer 2003, 94-5). According to Archer, in internal conversations we alternate between subject and object, but there is still some simultaneity between them: "first there is the subject's 'premonitory' notion, then her articulated thought-object, followed by the subject's reactions and then revisions" (ibid., 98). Thus, it is a cyclical model where one, for example, asks oneself questions and answers them.

Internal dialogue is prone to arise when we are unsure "about ourselves in relation to our circumstances" (ibid.,104). We can also converse with other people in our heads, but their "utterances" are always ours because we put the words in their mouths. Such conversations are always imaginary. However, it should not be forgotten that this capacity to "mind other minds" is originally based on very concrete abilities: for example, detecting intentionality and the eye-direction of others and also being able to share attention with others (Baron-Cohen 1995, 32-55). In Archer's conception it is not only with others that we converse, because we also encounter practical and natural orders while acting, and these concerns have to be dealt with. One thus gets the impression that because these are not social "orders," the actor deals with them in a non-social way.

The problem is that "the internal conversation can too readily be colonised by the social," and Archer claims that this was "Mead's path" (ibid., 117). I hope to have already shown that no such colonization actually took place with Mead, because the social in the form of the generalized other does not colonize anything; it enables one to have a unified self with the capacity for rational thought. Alongside other pragmatists – especially Peirce – Mead had a dialogical understanding of the self and of the whole process of human reasoning. Action normally proceeds through habitual ways of acting but the ever-changing nature of the world, i.e., the environment of action, forces us to ponder upon our responses and to change our habits – to solve problems inferentially and creatively (cf. Joas 1996). Both Mead and Peirce maintained that inferences arise all the time in the form of mental associations, and rationality has to do with reviewing these associations critically. For this reviewing to happen, one needs a mind and a self. An inner conversation can proceed through taking the roles of specific others but, as I already implied, in the case of adult human beings the usual suspect is the generalized other. It is what enables abstract and impersonal, objective thinking. This does not mean some sort of colonization by the social, because there is always unpredictability and novelty in the response of the actor: "response of the 'I' is something that is more or less uncertain" (Mead 1967, 176). The "I" is the response of the actor to those social attitudes that he or she takes on in the habitual and conventional "me." This response also changes those organized attitudes in turn (ibid., 196). The "I" is then the impulsive and novel side of action and the motor behind social change.

The interest in internal conversation is not restricted to mere psychological concerns. Archer (2003, 130) argues that reflexive deliberations in the form of internal conversations constitute a mediating process between structure and agency, because. structures affect action via internal conversations. Actors, then, deliberate in their internal conversations about structural topics, and this is the process through which structures actually affect actors. Actors do indeed take different attitudes toward structural factors – a useful reminder of the fact that structures do not always affect people in the same manner. Some people, for example, are more eager to adjust to social expectations than others. Structures are not something hovering above our heads and dictating our every move without our realizing their presence. This does not mean that actors could mould the structural circumstances as they please but, nevertheless, constraining and enabling structural aspects are activated through the projects actors pursue. Without such projects the structural properties "remain real, but their causal powers are unexercised" (ibid., 131). As real but unexercised powers, structures only mould the circumstances or environments of action.

It is plausible then to claim that actors do have internal conversations and that these conversations comment on structural aspects in one way or another (although there are no autonomous discussants in this "conversation"). Thus, one can say that actors' internal deliberations do mediate structures and action and also that structures affect actors through the intentional action processes that they choose to pursue. Contrary to what sociologists sometimes imply, structures do not affect everyone in the same manner, and Archer's intention is to show that actors take different types of reflexive stances toward structures (Archer 2003, 153 ff.). However, to assume that structural aspects would *always* be topics of discussion (internal or external) is not plausible.

What is even more important is that structural properties are activated not only when people are planning conscious projects of action, but also in their habitual modes of acting. Actually, the most abiding structures are those that are maintained in habitual action and seldom (or never) enter into discourse. Habits are not the same thing as rules or knowledge but dispositions that are in a probable manner manifested in certain environments. Habitual dispositions do not just mould the environments or circumstances of action but also affect that very action as habitualized action responses. Such is how habits are actualized in practice. Habits are not, then, only restrictive factors but also "positive agencies:" "The more numerous our habits the wider the field of possible observation and foretelling" (Dewey 2002, 175). This means that habits enable different lines of action, even lifestyles or "careers," and they usually also economize the need for reflexive monitoring. Bourdieu's notion of habitus comes close to this idea if we understand habitus as a bundle of habits that are systematically related to different fields.

From the pragmatist perspective, only those aspects of action enter discourse that are, for some reason or another, problematic for the actor. It is this problematic situation, i.e., the inhibition of action due to changes in the environment, that makes reflection possible. Then one has to deliberate reflexively and stage a dramatic rehearsal in one's imagination of different lines of conduct to foresee the possible consequences. Internal conversation is not a "foundational form of consciousness" but "the expression of a liquefaction of previously stable validities," as Joas (1985, 82) states in locating the psychic realm in general. Pragmatism does not imply a functionalistic account of structures, but a functionalistic account of human deliberation. Action is a cyclical process in which conscious deliberation usually arises only when necessary, i.e., when the habitual course of action encounters problematic situations. Then we are unsure "about ourselves in relation to our circumstances," as Archer (2003, 104) herself notes. Structural factors can also be topics of internal and external conversation, but this is not the "normal case." When structures enter conversations, they are usually about to be changed in some way by the actors concerned. Of course, this need not always be the case because actors might as well decide that the structures are worth maintaining. In many cases the habits are also so deeply ingrained that the actors concerned might not be able to call into question these structural elements properly. As emergent properties of action, structures are not functionalistic solutions, because they are cumulative causal processes that do not have any aims or purposes in their own right.[26]

Conclusion

The importance of practice implies that "what is central to human beings are not 'meanings,' but 'doings'" (Archer 2000, 189). In Archerian practice theory this implication is a challenge to the "hegemony of language." However, one has to choose between meanings and doings only if one is committed to a language-centered view of meaning. In the pragmatist perspective not all meanings are linguistic – and this is the real challenge to those who are voting for the hegemony of language. Still, there is no action without meanings and vice versa (see Kilpinen, forthcoming). Habitual dispositions are the prime example of such non-linguistic meanings. The human specialty is the intersubjective nature of meanings, that of shared meanings, which is based on taking the attitude(s) of others, as I have tried to argue. This attitude-taking is still usually habitual in the normal adult, and only problematic and/or conflict situations compel the actor to reflect on the expectations of other people. The concept of role conflicts comes close to this idea.

Practice theory goes astray if it claims that what is natural is somehow ontologically opposed to sociality. In fact, our social relations *are* our natural relations, or our natural way of being. So much so that sociality – in the sense of being able to think of other minds – precedes the ability to think of one's own mind in a reflexive manner. Personal identity then does not precede social identity in the manner that Archer would like to have it. This is something that is validated by many studies on the subject (e.g., Bogdan 2003; Baron-Cohen 1995), and Archer is not able to offer any viable theoretical options to conclude otherwise. To be self-conscious then is to be able to relate to oneself as an object. This does not preclude the possibility of a "proto-self" that monitors visceral reactions, for example (Damasio 2000).

In fact, a sense of self as we know it is precisely what is lacking in subjects who are not capable of entering social, intersubjective relations with shared meanings in contrast to mere interactive relations with the world. The case of autistic persons proves this point. Autists do not have normal, social relations with others, and this is

---

[26] One can still argue alongside Mead that societal arrangements can and should be subjected to scientific analysis so that we might be able to determine to what degree they enable the self-realization of the affected parties. If one's conception of selfhood is social, then this self-realization does not have to be opposed to the individuality of others.

why they also lack a unified self or self-consciousness in the sense of being able to see themselves through the eyes of others. As Oliver Sacks (1995, 190-191, 207-208) explains (though not in Meadian vocabulary), autists lack a generalized other as a constituent of unified selfhood, which means that their particular experiences remain as they are, chaotic particulars without any integration with each other. Thus, they usually – and very sadly – lack a coherent personal identity. Mead's insight is that before we have a unified, autobiographical self, we become social beings. In modern parlance, we become intersubjective instead of merely interactive beings. This distinction has traditionally gone unnoticed in sociology and, unfortunately, realist practice theory joins this tradition.

One also has to remember that certainly everything is not just discourse as the common social constructionist mantra would like to have it. Discourse is a phenomenon taking place within action processes, and its occurrence is in need of an explanation and not something to be taken for granted – and this applies to both internal conversations and societal discourses. It is the non-conscious habitual and bodily basis of action that has to be our starting principle for a theory of action and not just a residual category (cf. Camic 1986). Even if we place the mind within the action process, there is no reason why one could not still be a realist (as are all of the classic pragmatists).[27] External objects "possess certain characteristics by virtue of their relations to his [the individual's] experiencing or to his mind," but external objects are still "independent of the experiencing individual" (Mead 1967, 131).

Having said all of this, one can still be in full accordance with Archer's idea that structures are an emergent property of action. Social structures are not then to be located only in individuals or in individual actions because they are already in place when actors are born. Still they are realized through action and do not exist in some cultural ether that would fly above our heads. One can also whole-heartedly embrace such theories where practice occupies the central place. Practice is indeed "a learning process through which the continuous sense of self emerges" (Archer 2000, 122), *but* it is as social a process as there ever was. This is because self-consciousness is about being an object to oneself – not just an acting subject. One should thus be careful in not to overdo the practice approach with an undersocialized conception of man. I will let Mead have the last word: "We must be others if we are to be ourselves" (Mead 1925, 292).

---

27 Richard Rorty has portrayed pragmatism as an anti-realist endeavor, which relates to his view of pragmatism a precursor to the so-called linguistic turn. This interpretation is simply false because the pragmatist theory of meaning does not say that meanings *only* have to do with language. See Kloppenberg (1996) and Colapietro (2004b).

CHAPTER 3

Not by Rules or Choice Alone: A Pragmatist Critique of Institution Theories in Economics and Sociology[28]

Pioneering authors in the social sciences have defined their disciplines as sciences of institutions, including Émile Durkheim in sociology and Thorstein Veblen in economics. However, it is often unclear what is really meant by the term. This can lead to problematic presuppositions. Durkheimian sociology, for example, is related to a project that tries to show the limited scope of economic rationality. Durkheim argued that action does not happen in a social vacuum, which means that the institutional context of action cannot be omitted. Durkheim's argument came to be known as the classical sociological critique of economics. However, Durkheim conceptualized institutions as specifically normative in character, which is by no means the only way, or an unproblematic way, to approach institutions.

In this article the focus is on different institutional conceptions in both economics and sociology (mainly on the latter). According to W. Richard Scott (2001, 51-58), these conceptions can be classified into "regulative," "normative," and "cultural-cognitive" theories. In all these theories, institutions are social rules that regulate or even enable interaction. Scott argues that these theories are complementary and form a continuum, from conscious rules to taken-for-granted and unconscious cultural scripts.

The regulative view concentrates on the regulative rules of institutions and the sanction mechanisms needed to enforce them. However, these need not be formal rules, such as laws (Scott 2001, 51-54). Normative institution theory claims that institutions do not necessarily need sanctions to hold together, thanks to social pressures and the internalization of value-laden norms. If values and related norms have been internalized successfully, then actors behave according to normative expectations, even in situations where there is no external surveillance.

---

28 This chapter was originally published in *Journal of Institutional Economics* (2008), 4:3, 351-373.

Scott's (2001, 57-58) third classification is cultural-cognitive theory, which says that institutions are cultural scripts and common frameworks of meaning that do not need sanction mechanisms at all. Rather institutions are taken-for-granted knowledge schemas that constitute social reality. However, they are not just subjective beliefs because institutionalization takes place precisely when frameworks of meaning are seen as objective facts. In following pages, I will re-name cultural-cognitive views as "discursive theories" because these theories focus almost exclusively on the discursive dimension (whereas cultural-cognitive phenomena are not exclusively discursive). Risto Heiskala (2007) has suggested a fourth classification, which he calls pragmatist institutionalism.[29] I call this line of institutional theory "habitual institutionalism" since it uses habit and habitualization as its basic concepts. By taking habits properly into account, we end up with a broad institutional definition wherein institutions are not only common frameworks of meaning but also such habitual dispositions – not rules – of whose existence people might not be discursively aware. The habitual line of thinking about institutions is based on pragmatist philosophy.

My focus is on the basic ideas of these different institutional theories. This discussion unavoidably leads to some simplifications and not all relevant literature on the subject can be addressed. However, I am not content simply to classify different institutionalisms with Scott's apparatus (as Scott himself mainly is). Mere classificatory interest would go against the grain of pragmatism, as John Dewey (1910, iv), the classical pragmatist explains: "the pragmatic spirit is primarily a revolt against that habit of mind which disposes of anything whatever (...) by tucking it away, after this fashion, in the pigeon holes of a filing cabinet." The plot of this article is that each institutional theory can be approached as an answer to problems of the previously discussed theory.

This comparison is motivated by the view that habitual institutionalism offers solutions to some crucial difficulties in other institutional theories. These problems are: 1) treating institutions as a result of purely rational-calculative choices; 2) the subjugation of meaning to norms; and 3) the subjugation of meaning to discursive knowledge. In addition there is the tendency of over-emphasizing rules as the foundational feature of institutions. This tendency is also shared by some features of habitual institutionalism. Instead of rules, I will emphasize the role of habitual dispositions. On the whole, the habitual perspective does not imply that we have to abandon the insights of other institutionalisms altogether because institutions manifest regulative, normative and discursive aspects. These aspects are properly actualized when habitual action meets obstacles during its course due to changes in the environment of action. This environment is usually comprised of institutional factors.

---

29 Scott (2001, 58 n4) mentions a fourth institutional view which he calls cathetic or emotional. However, this is only an aside in Scott's discussion.

Regulative Institutionalism

The last three decades of the twentieth century showed signs that economists might, after all, take seriously the classical sociological critique that even economic actors never operate in an institutional vacuum. These signs appeared in the context of New Institutional Economics.[30] Much new institutionalism is in a complementary relationship with neoclassical economics (Swedberg & Granovetter 2001, 15), and accordingly some new institutionalists argue that individuals maximize their utility on the basis of given preferences. Nevertheless, new institutionalists also claim that actors always have cognitive constraints. New institutionalism also differs from neoclassical economics with respect to the expenses of buying and selling. The latter usually supposes that buying and selling takes place without cost. In this supposition the costs of getting information and maintaining an environment for economic action go unnoticed. This point has been especially discussed in transaction cost economics (Williamson 1985).

Some economists and economic historians try to integrate many sources of institutional analysis (e.g. Greif 2006). The work of Douglass C. North deserves special attention because his work has been an important inspiration to theorizing institutions within economics.[31] According to North (1990, 3), institutions are "the rules of the game in a society or, more formally, [they] are the humanly devised constraints that shape human interaction." Institutions mold interaction by structuring incentives for political, social, and economic exchange. They reduce the uncertainty of social interaction so that actors know how to act in different situations. Institutions can be either formal or informal constraints. Formal constraints are consciously devised rules whereas informal constraints are conventions and codes of conduct. Formal constraints are based on informal constraints, but the latter also supplement the former. The formal view is in keeping with common sense, since it is common to evoke institutions in the context of legally-binding rules and other such formal statutes.[32]

For regulative theorists it is obvious that individuals sometimes violate rules. That is why "an essential part of the functioning of institutions is the costliness of ascertaining violations and the severity of punishment" (1990, 4). It is also important for this theory corpus to define institutions as constraints on action that individuals have enacted upon themselves. Thereby new institutionalism can be formulated as a

---

30 New institutionalism has also been discussed, e.g., in economic history (North 1990), economic sociology (Brinton & Nee 1998), political science (Aranson 1998), and in anthropology (Ensminger 1998). Due to space restrictions, I will not be able to discuss all forms of new institutionalisms.

31 North has also discussed ideologies and belief systems, which makes his understanding of action more refined than in neoclassical economics (Denzau & North 1994). However, North's view of institutions has remained somewhat unchanged.

32 However, there are difficulties in maintaining a clear distinction between formal and informal rules (Hodgson 2006, 149-152).

project complementary to the choice theoretical approach of neoclassical economics. The fact that institutions are human creations implies that institutional theory has to begin with individuals, North (1990, 5.) argues. However, North's reasoning can be questioned because postulating a general "social constructionism" (institutions are human creations) does not automatically entail methodological individualism and rational choice theory (institutions come down simply to choices made by individuals).

An attentive reader can also find a new institutionalism in sociology, one that favors a regulative perspective on institutions. *The New Institutionalism in Sociology*, edited by Mary Brinton and Victor Nee, confronts Talcott Parsons' influential institutional theory in sociology (Nee 1998, 1). According to Nee, this means taking a choice theoretical perspective that explains how institutions are reproduced and sustained. The Parsonian tradition cannot explain this reproduction because it only presupposes the existence of institutions (I will address Parsons in the next section of this article). Like its counterpart in economics, sociological new institutionalism does not take rational choice at face value since it suggests that individuals make their choices within context-dependent constraints. Individuals then act intentionally, and they also calculate their utilities, but this is done in a world of incomplete information, incomplete mental models, and within limits set by transaction costs. Rationality is, to a certain extent, "bounded." Interests are also defined so broadly that actors can strive for purely social commodities, such as a favourable status position (Nee & Ingram 1998, 31). Nee (1998, 8) defines institutions as follows:

> Institutions, defined as webs of interrelated rules and norms that govern social relationships, comprise the formal and informal social constraints that shape the choice-set of actors. (…) They specify the limits of legitimate action in the way that the rules of a game specify the structure within which players are free to pursue their strategic moves using pieces that have specific roles and status positions.

New institutionalists in economics are particularly fond of using the metaphor of game rules when referring to institutions. However, new institutionalism in sociology is close to its counterpart in economics in aspects other than using the same metaphor. Rational action theory fundamentally characterizes both schools of thought. Sociological new institutionalism stresses that rationality is not only constrained by the imperatives of the market context and psychological deficiencies but also by normative factors. Economists have tried to discuss norms (e.g. Eggertsson 1991, 282) but, according to Nee and Ingram (1998, 21-22), they have not theorized them satisfactorily. This is where the possibility for a contribution by new institutional sociology lies.

Economists, as well as sociological new institutionalists, presume that it is rational for individuals to follow institutionalized regulative rules and to co-operate with others because of the fear of sanctions. However, this presumption cannot explain how rational actors originally come together and reach an agreement on the rules that are to be institutionalized (Beckert 2002, 29). If the fear of sanctions is the only thing that prevents institutions from falling apart, this makes institutions very unstable. Extensive social monitoring of action is possible only in relatively small groups, and "free riding" is always a tempting option even in these instances. Therefore, the power of sanctions is insufficient as an explanation of institutions if the theory does not also tell how institutions can arise out of purely individual motivations and how they are maintained on this basis.[33] An alternative way to formulate this critique has been suggested by Field (1981). He argues that one cannot avoid appealing to social structures that transcend individual interests. In his words, "there is a 'noneconomic bottom' we eventually ground on" (ibid., 193). This critique has often led to a normative conception of institutions.

Normative Institutionalism

As I stated above, Durkheim defined sociology as the science of institutions. His sociology was a science of secular morality that postulated what institutional factors were needed for social integration in a modern society. Durkheim was not interested in the efficiency of the economy but rather in its effects on the reproduction of the social order. For example, he wanted to "determine the function of the division of labour, that is to say, what social needs it satisfies" (Durkheim 1933, 45). He argued that societal development has gone hand in hand with the growing deregulation of economic affairs, which in turn has led to the weakening of moral ties. However, lasting economic relations cannot develop if based solely on selfish interests. According to him, egoistic actors could only establish very unstable institutions, something akin to a hidden state of war.

Institutions are at the center of Durkheim's critique of economics, and he examined them from the perspective of their functional regulation of economic relations, so that a normal or an "anomie-free" social order could develop in modern capitalism. For Durkheim, institutions are general, socially binding, and external to individuals. They constrain social action but they should not be understood as contracts made by individuals, because society is a fact that precedes individuals and is thus transcendent in relation to individuals. This is in clear contradiction to regulative theories. Furthermore, the regulation of economic affairs is functionally necessary for society, and therefore institutions always manifest a certain normative order.

---

33   There are also game-theoretical models that hold on to rational choice theory and try to explain the genesis of rules on this basis. Sugden (1995), for example, argues that conventions arise spontaneously in repeated games. These models, however, usually lack detailed notions of social structures (i.e., institutions). As Hodgson (2007, 218) argues, "game theory can never explain the elemental constraints or rules themselves."

Along with Durkheim Talcott Parsons is another major representative of classical sociological normative institution theory, although Parsons did not regard himself as a representative of any "ism" related to institutions. For matters of convenience, I will call Parsons and Durkheim Old Institutionalists in sociology. Parsons' explicit aim was to develop a synthesis of the classical works of social theory (Parsons 1949). These classical theorists were Alfred Marshall, Vilfredo Pareto, Émile Durkheim and Max Weber. Parsons argued that these authors "converge" on the main issues of action theory. It was his intention to show how the insights of these classics could be synthetized into a voluntarist action theory that also explained how individuals are motivated to act co-operatively. The main difference between Parsons and Durkheim is that Durkheim's institutionalistic sociology is overtly critical toward economics, whereas Parsons' view of sociology – as an analysis of economic institutions – is complementary to neoclassical economics (Velthuis 1999).

Parsons' *The Structure of Social Action* (published in 1937) discusses whether co-operative relations and social order can arise out of purely calculative rationality. He argued that the utilitarian model of economics guarantees the autonomy of actors because actors are seen as capable of choosing among different means. Thus, we have actors capable of voluntary action, but this model cannot explain how actors come to choose their goals or why they act co-operatively. This is the dilemma of regulative institutionalism that I presented above. Parsons' solution was to combine the elements of both voluntarist action and normativity in his own theory. This he tried to accomplish with his *unit act* concept consisting of goals, at least two means to achieve those goals, situational conditions, a normative orientation, and an actor. Neoclassical economics takes into account different situational conditions and the immediate goals of the actor but it does not discuss normative orientation. Normative orientation is a factor that directs individuals to act co-operatively so that the utilitarian problem of social order can be avoided. Instead of normative orientation, we can talk of social institutions that regulate action normatively because they are grounded on an authority originating in social values (Beckert 2002, 139).

Despite the fact that Parsons stressed the centrality of action, already present in his early work there is the idea of methodological holism because the integration of society is caused by common values, which are independent of action. In his later work, this holism leads to structural functionalism where the basic unit of analysis is the social system. However, there is no great rupture between the different periods of Parsons' work since the essential role of shared values and norms is his leitmotif (Turner 1991, xl-xlii).

There is also an Old Institutionalism in sociologically-oriented organizational analysis, which is heavily influenced by a Parsonian view of action and institutions. Its argument is that values, norms, and attitudes have effects on the institutionalisation of organizations. The main theoretician of this tradition is Philip Selznick, who was influenced by both Parsons and Robert Merton, his teacher (Scott, 2001, 22-24). Selznick focuses on the institutionalization of organizations, which takes place when organizations are taken as valued goals in themselves. Newcomers go through a socialization process that leads to the internalization of organizational values. These values manifest themselves in a commitment to the operations of the organization as a value in itself. (DiMaggio & Powell 1991, 14-15.) Organizations are thus comprised of an official, formal structure, which is supposed to act in an instrumentally rational sense, and of an informal structure, which can hinder or promote the operations of the formal structure. The formal structure is the "environment within and in relation to which the informal structure is built" (Selznick 1966, 251).

The essential difference between normative institution theories and regulative views is that, according to the former, institutions do not need any sanctions to back them up if values and norms have been succefully internalized in socialization. In this case individuals act in accordance with normative expectations even in contexts where there is no external monitoring of action. Thus norms and values motivate the actors to orient themselves co-operatively (Heritage 1984). In contrast to rational choice theories, actors do not have a calculative attitude in relation to these motivating factors, that is, the morally binding rules and institutions (Parsons 1949, 403). Normative institutionalism accordingly tries to narrow down the explanatory domain of mere calculative rationality. Its limitation, however, is related to the remedy that it offers, namely the stress on normative factors. All versions of normative institutionalism also presuppose that action is always understandable to actors, and only its acceptability varies. This leads one to presuppose a normative consensus at the societal level. However, values and meanings cannot be separated from each other in the way that normative institutionalists suggest. This separation results in a situation in which the actors' own apprehension of action is excluded. Normative institutionalism is incapable of discussing the knowledgeability of actors because of its focus on societal norms (cf. Giddens 1986, xv n1). This argument has been brought forward especially in the New Institutionalism of organizational analysis that argues for the role of institutions as a discursive resource.

Discursive Institutionalism

The starting point for new institutionalism in organizational analysis has been the finding that practices and arrangements are surprisingly similar from one organization to another. This does not necessarily imply a normative consensus, since institutions can be taken for granted for purely cognitive reasons; actors tend to think as they believe others think. They also tend to take for granted these social ways of thinking.

DiMaggio and Powell (1991, 9-11), who sketched a research program for new institutionalism in organizational analysis, argue that rational choice theory should be discarded for three reasons. First, individuals do not choose freely among different institutions, habits, and norms. These things are usually taken for granted, thanks to socialization or habitualization. Whereas old institutionalism in sociology stressed the importance of socialization in this process, new institutionalism emphasizes the role of routines. Second, individuals' choices and preferences cannot be understood outside the cultural and historical framework in which they are embedded. The concept of embeddedness derives from Karl Polanyi but Mark Granovetter (1985) is mainly responsible for the resurgence of the concept. Not unnaturally, the interest in embeddedness easily leads to a focus on institutional arrangements, although this interest has inspired the whole field of economic sociology (Rizza 2006). Third, institutions are often resistant to change. This is a consequence of individuals not being capable of imagining alternatives to the predominant institutional arrangements. DiMaggio and Powell (1991, 11) suggest that institutions not only constrain individuals' choices, but also "establish the very criteria by which people discover their preferences." This means that institutions actually produce individuals' preferences, and therefore there is no "preferring" objects of choice outside institutional frameworks.

DiMaggio and Powell also discard functional explanations in which institutions are seen as efficient solutions to problems of governance. In fact, the opposite of efficiency seems often to rule because institutions can prevent instrumentally efficient solutions. The old institutionalists in organizational analysis agreed on the relevance of this observation, but new institutionalists add the corollary that institutions are cultural-cognitive classifications. More specifically, institutions are taken-for-granted rules, classifications, scripts, and common belief systems (Scott 2001, 39). The main reason for these differing presuppositions can be found in the so-called cognitive turn that is also known as the cultural turn (DiMaggio & Powell 1991, 15). Here cognition refers both to rational thought as well as to its pre-conscious foundation such as representations and schemas. This is all very well, but I argue that in this line of thinking, the "cultural-cognitive" comes down to discursive classifications and schemas. The realm of the cultural-cognitive, however, is not exhausted with this particular use of the term, as I will argue in the next section.

At the level of action theory, the discursive turn has meant a move away from Parsonian theory toward ethnomethodology, phenomenological sociology, and cognitive psychology. DiMaggio and Powell explicitly seek an action theoretical foundation for their institutionalism in Garfinkel's ethnomethodology and in Peter L. Berger and Thomas Luckmann's phenomenologically inspired social constructionism (ibid., 19-22).

DiMaggio and Powell argue that Berger and Luckmann's (1995) view of institutions as reciprocal typifications of habitual action resembles Parsons' conception of institutionalized roles. Berger and Luckmann's analysis, however, operates at the level of discourse and knowledge, whereas Parsons highlights the normative aspects in the internalisation of role expectations. It is useful to take a closer look at the theory of Berger and Luckmann because it has been very influential in contemporary social sciences. They argue that any human activity necessarily becomes habitual when it is repeated frequently (ibid., 70-71). Habitualization means that action acquires an established form and becomes mere routine. The psychological benefit of habitualization is in reducing the need to choose, so that humans can act "with a minimum of decision-making most of the time" (ibid., 71). Action is characterized by habitualized routines instead of incessant pondering and selection among different options. Berger and Luckmann derive institutionalization from the effects of habitualization; institutionalization occurs when "there is a reciprocal typification of habitualised actions by types of actors. Put differently, any such typification is an institution" (ibid., 72). Thus, actors take institutions for granted because institutions are based on routine-like typifications.

Other actors appear as typifications in interaction, and the actor himself is seen as a typification. In addition, the interaction situations are usually typified (Berger & Luckmann 1995, 45-46.) Typifications are then reciprocal role expectations, which Berger and Luckmann understood as knowledge because of the influence of phenomenology. This knowledge tells how different types act in typical interaction situations. Thus, one finds oneself in an institutionalized setting whenever the actors and the context of action are typified. Some action situations are more institutionalized than others but there is always an element of institutionalization present, even in very intimate settings (in relations between spouses, for example).

Berger and Luckmann's theory tends to cast institutions as products of typified knowledge. The authors also try to theorize factors outside knowledge, that is, unreflected acts and habits that do not have conscious interpretations. However, they encounter problems when discussing these non-conscious routines and their meaningfulness. How can routines not be conscious and still meaningful? Actually they cannot if we identify meaning with reflexive intentional acts, as Berger and Luckmann do (Heiskala 2003). They take for granted that habits and habitualization are originally based on conscious action. The actor is in principle transparent to himself in his interpretations of meaning, but this transparency is hindered by the objectification of social reality. This objectification alienates the actor so that he or she cannot perceive the social character of these interpretations. Fundamentally, Berger and Luckmann present a so-called "mind-first" explanation, which makes it difficult to take into account the bodily and non-conscious aspects of action. Mind-first explanations start from conscious activities and theorize action from this basis. However, with this starting point it is difficult to theorize habits that do not initially have an interpretation in consciousness. Even while Berger and Luckmann discuss action, their analysis comes down to typifications and knowledge schemas.

Along with Berger and Luckmann, DiMaggio and Powell (1991, 22-25) also discuss Giddens' structuration theory, for example, although Berger and Luckmann's argumentation provides the essential framework for new institutionalism in organizational analysis (cf. Meyer & Rowan 1991) and for other discursive theories of institutions. Obviously, not all discursive theories are directly influenced by Berger and Luckmann, but the problems that originate in over-emphasizing the role of knowledge are shared by all, even by theories that explicitly stress the role of practices (see e.g., Reckwitz 2002). Giddens (1986, 4-7) has argued that the way to get out of this theoretical dead-end is to distinguish between discursive and practical consciousness. However, his notion of practical consciousness is based on the "knowledgeability" or the tacit knowledge that actors have, and this leads to the same sorts of difficulties as Berger and Luckmann's theory. In addition, Giddens identifies habits with routines and with actual conduct when it might be reasonable to define habits as dispositions or as proclivities to act in a certain way in certain situations. Precisely such a definition is found in the action theory of classical pragmatism.

Habitual Institutionalism

Economists who worked in the U.S. in the first half of the twentieth century and emphasized the role of institutions are often grouped under the label "Old Institutionalism" (Rutherford 1996). It was mainstream economic theory and policy for approximately 30 years (Hodgson 2004, 258-259). I will focus on the main theoretical inspiration behind the school, namely, Thorstein Veblen (1857-1929), who was also responsible for importing the pragmatist theory of action into economics (although Veblen did not say so himself). Old institutionalism in economics is sometimes thought of as merely an extension of the German historical school. If we define institutionalism in this manner, there are good reasons for claiming that Veblen was not an institutionalist (Kilpinen 2004). However, the label institutionalist is so established in the case of Veblen that it can be used, if it is remembered that besides German historicism, Veblen was also influenced by pragmatist philosophy, Darwin's evolutionary theory, and instinct psychology (Hodgson 2004, 66). My presentation of Veblen does not touch on all of the themes in his thinking (on these, see, e.g., McCormick 2006). There are also other old institutionalists in economics who are worth remembering (Commons, for example). However, my focus is on Veblen and especially on his methodological writings on economics, because they prepared the ground for a habitual institution theory.

Veblen was highly critical of many presuppositions in economics. His main criticisms had to do with the hedonistic conception of the individual, the atomistic conception of society, and presupposing a false role for causality and teleology in explaining individual action and social processes (Kilpinen 2000, 192). I will concentrate on these issues because they help to understand Veblen's own, habitual view of institutions and action.

By hedonism is usually meant a postulate in utilitarian philosophy which states that seeking pleasure and avoiding distress are the sole factors motivating human action. According to Veblen, the problem with this view is not the postulation of wrong motives for action, but the supposition that action needs any motives *at all*. In utilitarian psychology man is a passive being who acts only when a negative or a positive stimulus drives him to do so (Veblen 1919, 73-74). In line with pragmatist philosophy, Veblen thought that man always already acts (ibid., 74). The motives for action do not precede action because they enter the scene in the middle of ongoing action processes. Therefore it is not useful to analyze only discrete actions and their motives as neoclassical economics is wont to do (ibid., 156, 158). Because of their understanding of the "human condition," neoclassical economists do not in fact analyze action (ibid., 78). The historical school also discussed humans as passive creatures (ibid., 58), and this is why Veblen's institutionalism is not an extension of this school of thought.

Second, methodological individualism easily leads to an atomistic conception of society whereby society is understood merely as the sum of independent individuals (Veblen 1919, 139). Methodological individualism – approaching social phenomena solely through individuals – can be justified as an explanation strategy (if interactions between individuals are included; see Hodgson 2007). This sort of individualism becomes problematic, however, when it turns into an *ontological* postulate that denies the existence of all phenomena "above" the individual level. This postulate fails to take into account that people always act under institutional effects, not in a vacuum. In contrast to Parsons, the enrichment of neoclassical action theory with the normative context is not enough (Kilpinen 2000, 197-198.) Veblen was not opposed to analyzing norms because he thought that institutions are also normatively binding. Instead of imperatives for action, he analyzed norms, mainly as inhibiting factors that help actors in selecting among different impulses. (ibid., 357-358; cf. Mead, 1934.)

Third, economics denies the continuity and teleology of action with the argument that every choice situation is a discrete event. For economics, the only place for teleological continuity is in social processes, as in Adam Smith's thesis of the invisible hand. (Veblen 1919, 151). Veblen thought that this thesis was an "animistic" remnant because it relates teleology to inanimate social structures. Structures are ongoing and cumulatively causal processes that do not have any teleology in and of themselves. However, to argue that action consists only of discrete choices is to deny the continuity and rationality of action. (Ibid., 60-61.)

All of these critiques can be applied to contemporary neoclassical economics and also to the new institutionalisms of economics and sociology. These disciplines argue that the analysis of action is about analyzing rational *choices*.[34] Furthermore, normative institutionalism shares this underlying view of rationality. What then is Veblen's view? To put it briefly, institutions are always based on habits (Veblen 1919, 77). This is why I propose to call Veblen's theory *habitual* institutionalism, but it is also possible to label it pragmatist institutionalism instead (see Heiskala 2007). Both Veblen and classical pragmatists argued that habit is a reasoned routine because habitual and intelligent aspects overlap and interact during the course of action (Kilpinen 2000, 200-201). Habitual dispositions are related to actions that have been repeated in stable contexts and therefore require only a minimal amount of conscious thought to initiate and implement (Wood et al. 2002; Quellette & Wood 1998). However, habitual actions are not just dead routines for the reason that they contain the idea of normative self-control; they help in drawing relevant inferences from action contexts ("seeing" the relevant context and acting upon it in a particular manner). This is because habits are *dispositions* that are activated due to environmental cues. Habits do not refer to action as such because this would lead one to think that habits cease to exist when the related action is stopped. "The essence of habit," according to Dewey (1922, 42), "is an acquired predisposition to *ways* or modes of response."

Action is then always bound to take place in a certain context that is often, however, unstable. When the objective situation, the environment of action, changes the actors have to adapt to this by rearranging their habitual behaviour. Unstable contexts, then, require conscious deliberation and thought (Wood et al. 2002). Changing environments are potential crises and can be emotionally very stressful, but they are also places for creative action because they require conscious deliberation (Joas 1996). Doubt motivates the attainment of belief. From C. S. Peirce onwards this doubt-belief theory of inquiry has been a characteristic feature of pragmatism (Liebhafsky 1993). However, as habits do not produce identical copies of themselves, there is always variation among habits. Sometimes this variation can produce novel solutions even in situations with no exogenous changes (cf. Feldman & Pentland 2003, 112). The creative instances (mismatches between habits and environments) can also lead to conscious changes being done on the environment instead of simply adapting one's habits. Even the changing of one's habits is achieved indirectly through modifying the conditions of action: "by an intelligent selecting and weighing of the objects which engage attention" (Dewey 1922, 20). It is fair to say that the environments of action and habits are mutually constitutive.

In the case of "human animals," the environments of action are, to a large extent, institutional. In addition, the institutional environment blends in many ways with the physical environment (cf. Sperber 1996, 115). The production and reproduction

---

34 New institutionalists in economics and sociology undoubtedly see these choices as "bounded" to some extent but the underlying view of rationality is still one that emphasizes discrete acts of choice.

of society is an ongoing process because as the environment of action is often changing, it makes people change their habits, which in turn has effects on the environment, that is, on the institutional structure. Institutions are thus based on established tendencies to act in a certain manner in a familiar environment. There are also individual habits, but social habits are of interest in the case of institutions. Social habits are the ones that are activated by similar surroundings in many actors. In this sense habits are shared, even though habits need not be perfectly identical to have (more or less) the same institutional effects. It is also important to remember that institutions not only restrict action but also enable it. Habits are "positive agencies" because they determine "the field of possible observation and foretelling" (Dewey 1922, 175), or in other words, the lines of conduct that we use in our dealings with the world.

The traditions of pragmatism and classical sociology have both been critical of utilitarian thought (which economists have treated as a methodological model). However, the difference is that traditionally, sociologists criticize the utilitarian solution to the problem of action and social order, whereas pragmatists are also critical of the utilitarian solution to the problem of action and *rationality* (Joas 1993, 18). Sociologists maintain that the utilitarian solution is not a real solution to the constitution of the social order, and therefore we need norms. To a certain extent this argument is powerful, but the view of rationality as unconnected acts of calculation remains untouched (Whitford 2002). The pragmatist notion of habits as building blocks of institutions reminds one also of more recent theorizing in sociology, especially of the work of Pierre Bourdieu and his concept of "habitus" (Bourdieu 2000). The habitus is a system of dispositions which structures (in Bourdieu's terminology) "fields" or institutions, since habitus is the subjective side of social positions. However, habit fares better as a general action-theoretical conception because the habitus is related to such particular institutions that are hierarchical and organized. I would argue, then, that Bourdieu's fields are indeed institutions – but not all institutions are fields. Only those institutions that are hierarchical and organized (at least to some extent) are fields. They include many organizations, for example.

Veblen's pragmatist theory of action took into account instincts as inherited dispositions, whereas habits refer to learned dispositions. As learned dispositions, habits belong to the realm of the cultural-cognitive (take notice that the term is now used in a broader manner than in the last section). Veblen argued that instead of a dichotomy, there is a continuum between instinctual and rational action because instinctual action is also intelligent and teleological (Veblen 1914, 30-31). Instincts provide somewhat abstract objectives for action, and therefore habits are needed to guide it. In other words, instincts can be realized through many different habits. The difference between animals and human beings is not that human beings alone are capable of goal-directed behavior (Bogdan 1994). The difference lies in the unique character of human consciousness, which is a trait developed in biological evolution and which can monitor instinctual dispositions due to its self-reflexive nature (Bogdan 2003). However, this character is still based on instinctual and habitual action (Veblen 1914, 6-7). There is often a positive feedback mechanism between instincts, habits and institutions so that institutions tend to reinforce those instincts and habits that are favorable to their existence (Brette 2003, 466). However, Veblen assimilated from William James the idea that instincts do not make us do anything; they are potentialities that have to join hands with impulses and habits to have any effects (Kilpinen 2000, 186).

Discursive institution theorists also use the concept of habit. For example, Scott (2001, 80) argues that institutions may be embodied in habitualized routines. However, for these theoreticians, habit is not reflexive in the same manner as it is for Veblen and for pragmatists. For discursive institution theories, habituality and rationality take turns in the course of action, whereas for pragmatists habitual behavior and consciousness are not mutually exclusive. In fact, habit and reason or habit and rational consciousness are *overlapping* phenomena. This means that habits are not mere dead routines. "Deliberation is rational," as Dewey (1922, 198) explained, "in the degree in which forethought flexibly remakes old aims and habits." Therefore, rationality is "not a force to evoke against impulse and habit" (ibid., 196). Rational thought is not the antithesis of habits as such, although inflexible habits – "enslavement to old ruts" (ibid., 66) – can become a problem.

Berger and Luckmann derive habit from action that is originally conscious, that is, from conscious knowledge. For them, action is first and foremost conscious but it happens that some acts are repeated often enough so that they sink below consciousness and turn into habitual typifications. Pragmatists think that in many cases the opposite is true: conscious action derives from habitual action. This is because people tend to respond habitually to familiar stimuli without ever having consciously considered their responses. Deliberation enters the scene when the stimuli change or in cases where the stimuli stay the same but the responses prove to be inadequate for some reason or another (the same stimuli with contextual changes).

Parsons did a disservice to sociology by taking habit out of the conceptual arsenal of the discipline (Camic 1986). He wanted to avoid any theorizing resembling behaviorism and thus eliminated also pragmatism. However, neither Veblen nor the classical pragmatists were behaviorists for the simple reason that consciousness still plays a role in their constructions. Consciousness is not regarded as the primus motor but, instead, as a steering apparatus that guides behavior through conflicting stimuli. Old institutionalism in economics was incompatible with Parsons' grand project, whose goal was erecting theoretical foundations for an independent science of sociology that would exist alongside economics. Veblen did not agree that institutions could be left for sociology to deal with, and his thought endangered the idea of a strict division of labor between economics and sociology. (Camic 1987, 428-429.)

Richard Rorty was a famous spokesperson for pragmatism or "neopragmatism." He argued that pragmatism is an anti-realistic and anti-representationalist undertaking. His interpretation had the unfortunate consequence of dissolving the essential features of pragmatism and turning it into a form of discursive institutionalism. My reading of pragmatism is more in line with those authors who see it as a theory of action that is based on the habit-concept and on situated creativity (Joas 1993, 1996; Kilpinen 2000, 2003, 2004; Whitford 2002). Moreover, I argue that classical pragmatism is based on a form of philosophical realism.[35] This form of realism argues that the environment of action bears on ongoing action processes in the sense that those stimuli that relate to these processes are the ones that get picked out from all the rest (Gronow 2008a).

Veblen was not only critical of neoclassical economics but also of Marxian theory (Hodgson 2001, 140-141). Marxian theorists have a tendency to think of actors "economistically", as knowledgeable interest-calculators just as neoclassical economists do. However, the basic premise of Marxism is to explain individual behavior through its social or economic context. This results in treating psychology as redundant. In contemporary parlance we can say that Veblen criticized both methodological holism and methodological individualism. The former loses sight of action if it argues for a supposedly independent social level, and it cannot explain how this level is connected with individuals (Hodgson 2004, 27-28). As an ontological postulate (only individuals exist), the latter fails to see the fundamental sociality of human undertakings. The evolution of individuality also has to be explained causally; it should not simply be treated as a given as neoclassical theorists tend to do. The evolution of individuality led Veblen to adopt a process explanation that takes biological factors into account as well as socio-economic ones.

However, Veblen did not reduce all explanations of social phenomena to biology, as some of today's evolutionary psychologists try to do. Hodgson has suggested that Veblen's philosophy of science was affected by Conwy Lloyd Morgan's conception of emergent properties. A property is emergent if its existence and nature are dependent on lower level entities but it cannot be reduced to these or prefigured from them ad hoc. Morgan argued that socio-economic evolution takes place on an emergent level so that it cannot be accounted for by individuals' biological properties, nor does it require changes in these properties. Veblen added the essential insight of institutionalism according to which institutions are the proper objects of selection in socio-economic evolution, although he did not use the concept of emergent properties. (Hodgson 2001, 141-142.) Institutions then exhibit some variety; there is also

---

35 Haack (1993, 189) argues convincingly that "[d]eclining the irrealist option [i.e., Rorty's 'vulgar pragmatism' as she calls it] does not oblige us to go grandly transcendental. We may opt, instead, for a Peircean pragmatism, for a minimal or for a stronger realism." See also Rochberg-Halton (1986), Kloppenberg (1996), and Beckert (2003).

a selection process that is due to the environment of institutions. In addition, institutions embody "heredity," which Veblen explained with the mechanism of habits[36] (Hodgson 2004, 188-192). However, habits are never exact copies in the sense that genes tend to be (excluding occasional mutations) (cf. Sperber 1996).

Hodgson and Knudsen (2006, 14) argue that social evolution is not merely analogous to evolution in the natural world: "at a high level of abstraction, social and biological evolution share these [same] general principles." However, Darwinism merely offers a general framework which, in practice, needs to be replenished with more detailed explanations. In this general framework, all complex evolving systems exhibit the basic mechanisms of Darwinian evolution (variation, selection and heredity). These systems include institutions. Institutions are indeed complex and they evolve – sometimes gradually, sometimes in an abrupt manner – but one should be careful when using the system metaphor. It is by no means self-evident that institutions exhibit properties that characterize "proper" systems (e.g., organisms). A cautionary note is in order because enthusiasm for systems theories led Talcott Parsons to treat social structures as intentional beings that follow clearly defined goals. Fortunately, Hodgson does not project actual intentions onto institutions, and he soundly argues that institutions are open systems.

Hodgson (2006, 138) defines institutions as "systems of established and prevalent social rules that structure social interactions." He also emphasizes that rules should be understood as dispositions. However, if habits are the mechanism through which institutions are maintained, then the important issue concerns non-conscious *dispositions* instead of rules. Rules are related to dispositions – but dispositions can be present without proper rules behind them. The uniform and *rule-like* nature of many dispositions should not lead us to mistake them for rules. Hodgson maintains that institutions are always in principle codifiable as rules. Indeed, in some respects they are but in many cases this codification only takes place after someone acts against established habits. Hodgson wants to avoid defining institutions as behaviour because this would "mislead us into presuming that institutions no longer existed if their associated behaviours were interrupted" (2006, 139). This is an important observation, and I am not suggesting that we define institutions through behaviour. But I am not suggesting either that we define them through rules because this would lead us into thinking that institutions do not exist if no associated rules are to be perceived. Instead, we should define institutions through dispositions that are, for the most part, habitual. The habitual is the basic level of institutional reproduction – as Hodgson agrees – and not rules that are related to the discursive aspects of institutions. Defining institutions through rules draws a too uniform and mentalist picture

---

36 The variety of habits and possible selection mechanisms among varying habits can also be of interest to evolutionary social scientists (cf. Feldman & Pentland 2003).

of action. Therefore, my version of the institutional definition goes as follows: *institutions are established and prevalent social dispositions that structure social (inter)action.*

This definition deserves some clarification because not all dispositions are related to institutions, but only those are that are sufficiently established, one's that exhibit temporal constancy. This is not to deny that minor transformations can be frequent (cf. Sperber 1996). However, an institution that is completely transformed overnight simply is not the same institution anymore. Institution-related dispositions are also prevalent; they are *social* ways of responding to environmental cues and not just individual habits. Habits come to be shared through socialization but this socialization does not have to be explicit teaching or schooling on the correct ways of doing things. More often than not, the socialization of habits takes place through the absorption of implicit expectations that are met in different contexts. This absorption is made possible by the intersubjective nature of human cognition; in Meadian vocabulary one can argue that proper selfhood is born through taking the role of the other toward oneself (Mead 1934; Gronow 2008a). In normal human beings the process of learning habits is also more or less habitual and not something that needs to be explicitly taught. I have bracketed the "inter" in my definition of institutions because institutions also structure action when other actors are not present (though often with lesser intensity). This fact is due to the intersubjective nature of selfhood. Institutions are, more or less, part of our selves as the "generalized others" that give things objective meanings (Mead 1934). This constitutive intersubjectivity accordingly implicates that the utilitarian dilemma of social order is more or less artificial.

Conclusion

In Table 1 are the main postulates of different institution theories. In the following section, I will not go into the Table's every detail, but instead I will focus on those differences between institutional theories that have a bearing on my main argument.

The regulative view concentrates mainly on legally sanctioned and other quite formal rules. These are seen to coerce individuals to behave in line with institutional ends because it is instrumentally rational for actors to do so (mainly due to fear of sanctions). Normative theorists argue that instrumental rationality is usually not applicable whenever moral issues enter the picture – and in the cases of institutions such issues always do enter in. These institutional norms weigh on actors' as moral obligations that have to be fulfilled. Discursive theorists, however, propose that even moral obligations are mainly cultural schemas. Therefore, they emphasize the nature of institutions as knowledge schemas that are common beliefs about the nature of social roles and action situations. It is an inherent property of the human psyche to form routines whenever these beliefs are taken as the orthodox conception of the social

Table 1. Institution Theories

	Regulative	Normative	Discursive	Habitual
The Discipline(s) of Institution theories	New Institutionalism in Economics and Sociology	Old Institutionalism in Sociology and Organizational Analysis	New Institutionalism in Organizational Analysis	Old Institutionalism in Economics (Veblen), Pragmatism
Basis of Compliance	Expedience	Social obligation	Taken-for-grantedness, shared understanding	Shared dispositions
Basis of Order	Regulative rules	Binding expectations	Constitutive schemas	Taken-for-granted ways of acting
Mechanisms	Coercive	Normative	Mimetic	Habitual
Logic	Instrumentality	Appropriateness	Orthodoxy	Pragmatic
Indicators	Rules, laws, sanctions	Proprieties, obligations	Common beliefs, shared knowledge	Habits
Basis of Legitimacy	Legally sanctioned	Morally governed	Recognizability, culturally supported	Proficiency of action

Revised from Scott (2001, 52).

world. Hence, actors tend to do as they believe others do (this is the mimetic aspect) and as they think has always been done.

Pragmatists would argue that one should not overdo the "thinking aspect" in action. That is, even humans do not often think about what they are doing; instead, they act on the basis of shared dispositions and reflect on their action if need be. Thus, rules are not necessary for the existence of institutions. It is the proficiency of habituated action in more or less stable environments that is important in understanding the reproduction of institutions. Furthermore, there is no deep divide between acting and thinking because a part of thinking process is in responding sensorimotorally to different objects, whether in images only or also in overt actions. However, invoking the habitual dimension should not act as a catch-all term that ends inquiry (cf. Perraton and Tarrant 2007). Habits can and should be studied, for example, through routines (Wood et al. 2002) or by taking metaphorical thought into account (cf. Lakoff & Johnson 1999).

From a pragmatist/Veblenian point of view, it can be maintained that institutions also have regulative, normative, and discursive aspects besides their habitual nature. Nevertheless, these other aspects are present in varying degrees and they tend to become habitual as well. One can, for example, have discursive notions that are habitual. In any case, it is useful to take into account the strengths of other institutionalisms. However, the habitual perspective is more comprehensive in its scope. This is because institutions are always based on habitual dispositions, whereas institutions sometimes can do without the regulative, normative and, discursive aspects. For example, in many Western societies institutional arrangements that are related to gender are nowadays mainly habitual (of course gender also has a biological basis).[37] For the most part, these arrangements are not regulated by laws. It is not proper, either, to label some professions unsuitable for women on moral grounds. Nevertheless, there are taken-for-granted discursive scripts related to gender roles, and there are certainly habitual ways of doing things that are difficult to call into question. In practice, all institutional aspects are usually present and often in varying degrees. However, I am arguing that the presuppositions of other institutionalisms should be reconciled with habitual institutionalism (and not the other way around). The remainder of my article is devoted to this task, but this attempt can only be preliminary, owing to the vastness of the area that should be covered.[38]

This reconciliation starts with treating the regulative institution theories' view of calculative rationality, not as the paradigm case of rationality, but rather as its special, though empirically frequent, instance. After Parsons, sociologists have been willing to admit that calculative rationality characterizes economic conduct and is therefore a natural presupposition for economics. However, rational choice is not even the paradigmatic form of economic conduct, but rather its special case that is caused by the crises of action situations in which habitual action confronts obstacles due to the changes in the environment of action. Even in such situations, action is still based on habitual dispositions because habits make conscious deliberation possible. Moreover, deliberation is not exhausted by calculating utilities based on stable preferences; values, norms, and beliefs have to be taken into account. Furthermore, institutions cannot be theorized exclusively from the perspective of rational choice, since stable, cooperative relations do not develop out of purely egocentric calculations (cf. Beckert 2002).

---

37 My thanks to Risto Heiskala for suggesting this example.
38 Fortunately, there are also other writers who cherish similar synthetic aims (their premises are not necessarily similar to mine). For example, the economic historian Avnir Greif (2006, 13) calls for "conceptual and analytical frameworks that integrate diverse lines of institutional analysis and accommodate the factors, forces, and considerations that each highlights."

Atomistic views of society downplay the fact that actors are fundamentally social in their make-up, that is, they take the attitudes of others toward themselves (see Mead 1934, 156; cf. Fontana et al. 1992). Methodological individualism can be acceptable as a *methodological* postulate if it only aims at highlighting the importance of individual action. There is no reason to turn this postulate into an ontological view according to which only individuals exist in society. Thus, one should not forget the social context of action but, in addition, it is useful to take notice of pragmatism's action theory, which constitutes a viable alternative to rational choice theories (cf. Beckert 2003, 770). The latter have focused on discrete acts and their motives at the expense of the continuity of action. Instead, attention should be paid to the way in which motives relate to the ongoing action process of the individual, to his or her habits and to the larger institutional context. Having said this, one can admit that institutions also have such regulative aspects that affect action via different explicit rules, laws, and sanctions.

Normatively oriented theoreticians often argue that successfully internalized institutions do not need sanctions to back them up. Well and good, but values and norms are not independent of the meanings and the interpretations attached to them, that is, independent of action processes. Value orientations are related to particular social contexts and on the projects that actors happen to be pursuing. These projects need not always be conscious, which means that *knowledge* is not the final word on the theme of meaning. The classical pragmatist emphasis on habitual action enables us to get rid of residual categories related to "tacit knowledge." Conscious deliberation regulates ongoing habitual conduct in problem situations but habits need not originally have an interpretation in consciousness. Furthermore, habits are not just dead routines since they are the very foundation on which reflection and consciousness are built on. Thus, the bodily and non-conscious aspects of action can be theorized more consistently in habitual institutionalism than in different social constructionisms, for example. It seems likely that most cognitive processes are not conscious – and this is not due to forgetfulness or "repression." To state the matter differently, all meaning should not be reduced to knowledge – and this is why the actor is not transparent to himself.

CHAPTER 4

Uneasy Bedfellows or Natural Allies? Bourdieu and Pragmatism

Pierre Bourdieu (1930-2002) left a body of social theory that continues to draw well-deserved and critical attention (see, e.g., Swartz 1997; Jenkins 2002; Calhoun et al. 1993; Shusterman 1999). There has been some controversy as to how his work should be approached because he had reservations about "grand theory." Bourdieu's most important concepts are those of habitus, field, and capital. Especially the notion of habitus will be the focus of this article. I will relate it to the concept of habit, as it is used in pragmatism. Pragmatism and Bourdieu shared an interest in the importance of practical and habitual action. Analyses of habitual action can be encountered in classical sociology (Camic 1986). However, the phenomenon of habituality is more central for the pragmatist tradition.

    Bourdieu's focus is on the correspondence between dispositions and social positions. Such a correlation is not present in all sociologically interesting research questions – not even all of those cases that are related to habitual action. Therefore I will argue that there is a need for both pragmatist notions of action and for Bourdieusian analyses of the way in which socioeconomic factors profoundly affect our relationship with the world. Bourdieu's theory is at its core a theory of societal power. In the social sciences, pragmatism has been discussed in relation to theories of action. However, pragmatists also have discuss other issues of social theory; pragmatism can be read as a commentary on the constitution of social order and on issues of social change. Furthermore, Bourdieu's theory was founded on empirical studies and never concentrated on pure theory. Pragmatists, for their part, often discuss very general issues concerning "the human condition" (though rarely in those very words). Thus, it can be admitted that a perspective that discusses action and structures on a fairly theoretical level does not do full justice to Bourdieu's comprehensive vision of sociology. However, it is to be remembered that Bourdieu (1998, vii) designated his theory as "a philosophy of action."

Brubaker (1993, 217) has suggested that "Bourdieu's work (…) is particularly ill suited to a conceptualist, theoretical, logocentric reading." The reason for this suggestion is that Bourdieu's core concepts are not unambiguous and precise. Brubaker argues further that Bourdieu was trying to develop a certain sociological disposition and this disposition is related to particular fields and the historical struggles being waged in these fields. Thus, Brubaker concludes that "[i]f sociological work is indeed governed by practical dispositions rather than theoretical logic, then there is no point in a purely theoretical reading of Bourdieu or anyone else" (ibid., 218). However, if one takes Bourdieu seriously then a purely theoretical reading is not even possible. It is, after all, our dispositions that do the reading. While discussing any theory, we certainly should be aware of their historical and doctrinal origin. Furthermore, Bourdieu's aversion towards grand theories is an attitude that can be embraced. The major fault with these sorts of theories is that they are guilty of intellectualism, that is, they mistake the models of reality for that reality (or are not interested in modeling this relationship). However, a similar mistake follows if one thinks that theories are only practical dispositions and therefore one can use them unproblematically in any kind of empirical research. When taken to the extreme, Brubaker's suggestions mean that only the "initiated" – those who have internalized the theory in question into their dispositions – are allowed to discuss anything. Such an attitude is problematic because if a shared habitus is our goal as researchers then "its products find confirmation and validation only too readily within the circle of sharers" (ibid., 224). One can certainly agree with Brubaker that the only way to test anything at all is in and through practice. This is also my intention. For a Bourdieusian, theory is, after all, a form of practice.

The structure of the text is such that first I discuss the similarities between pragmatism and Bourdieu; then I proceed to explicate the differences that certainly are there; the last section of the article is devoted to a discussion what can be learnt from the comparison previously made in the article. Bourdieu and the pragmatists (Dewey and Mead in particular) share an understanding of the importance of practical action. However, Bourdieu's notion of societal reproduction, and thus also his notion of structures, is thoroughly based on the idea of hierarchical divisions. Action theory is always related – at least in the social sciences – to notions of social structure. However, sociality is not necessarily restricted to issues of hierarchies. The pragmatist view (especially a Meadian view) argues that sociality is also about identifying with others; even with such others that do not share our habits. Thus, Bourdieu and pragmatism share many starting points but also disagree on the nature of sociality – but this disagreement can be taken as a sign of complementary perspectives.

Bourdieu in Context

Pragmatism never had a direct impact on Bourdieu's work, although the commonalities between his thinking and this thought tradition were (eventually) brought to his attention. In fact, some of the similarities are so obvious that one can only speculate as to how his theory would have turned out had Bourdieu acquainted himself with pragmatism in his formative years. Later on, Bourdieu explicitly admitted the existence of affinities between his thinking and that of John Dewey. Bourdieu thought that these "affinities and convergences are quite striking" (Bourdieu & Wacquant 1992, 122). Some scholars have tried to explain these similarities (see Ostrow 1990; Colapietro 2004a). For example, while discussing the affinities between Bourdieu and G. H. Mead, a classical pragmatist, Aboulafia (1999, 153-4) comes up with the following long list:

> a social conception of mind and agency; a penchant for non-positivistic approaches to the empirical sciences; a dedication to the interdisciplinary; views that link certain kinds of problem solving behavior to reflection; a commitment to giving the bodily and dispositional their due; a concern for lived, non-scientized, time; recurrent appeals to "open" systems, improvisation, and the role of conflict in change; a pluralistic vision; a preference for analyzing language in terms of use; an emphasis on reasonableness as opposed to a transcendental notion of reason; a willingness to speak the language of interest and a healthy suspicion regarding views from nowhere; an insistence on the importance of recognition in social life; and even a similar use of sports metaphors and analogies.

Aboulafia made an interesting suggestion that "Mead's [concept of] 'me' is comparable to Bourdieu's *habitus*" (ibid., 156). However, Aboulafia does not elaborate on the issues that this remark implies for the constituents of Bourdieu's habitus. It is quite surprising that the other scholars who take note of the similarities between Bourdieu and pragmatism have not really elaborated on them either (for example, Colapietro 2004a). Thus, regardless of the attention that Bourdieu's affinity with pragmatist thought has received, the discussion about it has been anything but exhaustive. Before going into this topic I will say something about the context of Bourdieu's thought.

One frequent criticism of Bourdieu's work has concerned the issue of economism. Reflecting on the reasons for this charge, Bourdieu had the following to say: "Paradoxically, the term interest has brought forward the knee-jerk accusation of economism" (Bourdieu & Wacquant 1992, 115). Bourdieu's way of using the notion of interest was actually "a deliberate and provisional reductionism that allows me [i.e., Bourdieu] to import the materialist mode of questioning into the cultural sphere from which it was expelled, historically, when the modern view of art was invented and the field of cultural production won its autonomy" (ibid., 116). Thus, art and culture in general have traditionally been viewed as disinterested and autonomous spheres but, in reality, they are symbolic fields with characteristic interests that differ from – and often contradict – economic interests. The very first sentence of *Distinction* is telling in this regard: "There is an economy of cultural goods, but it has a specific logic" (Bourdieu 1984, 1). In reality, economic interests are a subclass of social interests, defined by their own logic particular to this field. However, historically this economic field has developed a tendency to dominate other fields (ibid., 562). Economism would explain everything in connection with economic interests, and thus one can admit that Bourdieu's theory was different in this regard.

Sulkunen (2009, 24) states that Bourdieu's fondness for economic terms "must be understood as a provocation towards the labour theory of class, particularly its Marxist version that was widespread in the 1970s in Western social science and dominant in France." This is probably an apt contextualization – if one adds that Bourdieu is also arguing against Kantian aesthetics (Gronow J. 1997) and balancing on a tight rope between phenomenological and structuralist traditions. Sulkunen (2009, 24-5) also suggests that "[t]o have an interest is to accept and to understand the rules, structures and positions of the field." Bourdieu's concept of interest is so broadly defined that it actually indicates that people usually have a habitual understanding of their social environment. This is because action always takes place in relation to particular aspects of an environment. Usually those aspects of environments get picked out that feel familiar and are therefore also habitual. However, Bourdieu's point is that this relation is made possible by one's socioeconomic status: habitual dispositions (ways of relating to environments) correspond with social positions.

Circumstances are always an embodied part of us in the form of our habitus. This also means that we often fail to recognize the habit to which our habitus corresponds, with the exception that there can be mismatches between habitus and circumstances. Bourdieu (2000, 143) indeed argues that the "practical sense of action is a kind of necessary coincidence … between a habitus and a field (or a position in a field)." This emphasis on necessary coincidence has led to accusations of determinism (Jenkins 2002). However, Bourdieu himself stressed that it is not a mechanical determinism that he is after, but rather "conditioned and conditional freedom" (Bourdieu 1990a, 55), or "spontaneity without consciousness or will" (ibid., 56). He was trying to restore "a certain free play to agents, without forgetting, however, that decisions are merely choices among possibles, defined, in their limits by the structure of the field" (Bourdieu 2005, 197).

Converging on Habituality

Bourdieu has given many definitions for his concept of habitus; here is one early (and wordy) instance:

> The habitus, the durable installed generative principle of regulated improvisations, produces practices which tend to produce the regularities immanent in the objective conditions of the production of their generative principle, while adjusting to the demands inscribed as objective potentialities in the situation, as defined by the cognitive and motivating structures making up the habitus (Bourdieu 1977, 78).

Bourdieu's basic idea is that perception is always "diacritical:" it distinguishes some things from the environment and marks them as important (Bourdieu 1990b, 79). Our cognition thus consists of different principles of classification, division and hierarchization, and these principles are formed by our previous experiences, especially experiences related to socioeconomic background. The concept of habitus is meant to capture the way in which this practical engagement with the social world is inscribed in us, it is "society written into the body" (ibid., 63).

According to Bourdieu, the workings of the habitus are more or less unconscious because the incorporation of objective social structures takes place habitually (ibid., 78-9). As already mentioned, this incorporation works through past experiences, early life experiences in particular, which are inscribed in our bodies in the form of dispositional tendencies. The past is thus actively present in our practices, which consist of dispositions. This argument could indicate some sort of determinism, but Bourdieu (1990a, 56) thinks that it actually gives us relative autonomy in relation to the immediate action contexts that we encounter. The habitus is not intended to portray a "mechanical reaction, directly determined by the antecedent conditions" (Bourdieu 1977, 73). Thus, a purely mechanical application of a rule is not what he is after. The habitus is incorporated in "systems of perception, appreciation and action [which] enable them to perform acts of practical knowledge, based on the identification and recognition of conditional, conventional stimuli to which they are predisposed to react" (Bourdieu 2000, 138). These systems "generate and organize practices and representations that can be objectively adapted to their outcomes without presupposing a conscious aiming at ends" (Bourdieu 1990a, 53). With the help of concept of habitus, Bourdieu intended to "escape from under the philosophy of the subject without doing away with the agent ... as well as from under the philosophy of the structure but without forgetting to take into account the effects it wields upon and through the agent" (Bourdieu & Wacquant 1992, 122). Thus, he was trying to find out a way to situate his work in relation to both phenomenology and structuralism – but as a "third way" that transcends the problems of these alternatives.

Habitus is thus a dispositional factor that does not preclude improvisation. This dispositional character also goes for the concept of habit, as it is used by pragmatists. Pragmatism is a very general movement in philosophy and the human and social sciences. According to Westbrook (2005, xi), all pragmatists "believe that the truth of a proposition is to be judged by its consequences in experience." Accordingly, meaning is always related to action. This stress on practice is in alignment with Bourdieusian ways of thinking. The context of Bourdieu is, after all, such a practice theory that underscores bodily involvement with our surroundings. For example, Taylor (1993, 46) has situated Bourdieu in a Wittgensteinian tradition that opposes "the mind-set of the intellectualist." This mind-set sees rules everywhere and seeks secure, infallible, foundations for knowledge. Wittgenstein surely is a major figure in this tradition but, one can add, so are all of classical pragmatists. The role of beliefs is not to mirror the world as accurately as possible, without perspective, but to resolve problematic, practical action situations whenever they are encountered. These problem situations are experienced with our acting bodies, with our habits, not just through such things as "language-games," for example. Thus, one could argue that pragmatists are even more true to the practice agenda than Wittgenstein ever was.

The concept of habit is familiar in sociology and social theory. For example, both Durkheim and Weber used this concept extensively in their work (Camic 1986). Contemporary psychologists also recognize the effects of habits (e.g., Wood et al. 2002). Pragmatism, however, is exceptional in its extensive usage of the idea of habituality. In pragmatism, "habit" is a basic category of action, not a deviation from more proper forms of action. Habits refer to the fact that having done something previously is a reason for action and therefore action does not necessarily need any explicit motives. It can be reasonably argued that the habit concept is *the* unifying theme of the whole pragmatist tradition (Kilpinen 2009). As John Dewey maintained in his preface to *Human Nature and Conduct* (1922):

> an understanding of habit and of different types of habit is the key to social psychology, while the operation of impulse and intelligence gives the key to individualized mental activity. But they are secondary to habit so that mind can be understood in the concrete only as a system of beliefs, desires and purposes which are formed in the interaction of biological aptitudes with a social environment.

Social psychology and habits come first, while individualized beliefs, purposes, and so on, come only after them because the human organism is always interacting with its environment through bodily action – or actually "trans-acting." Dewey and Bentley (1949) argued that the concept of interaction presupposes independently existing "interactors," whereas trans-action (with a hyphen) indicates that no such independence exists (see also Lyng & Franks 2002). Action is always, and especially in its habitual phase, embedded in its environment but active engagement is also a factor which constitutes our environment. This trans-action is exemplified in habits because habits are "ways of using and incorporating the environment" (Dewey 1922, 15). Habits thus indicate that the circumstances are, to some extent, a part of us in our tendencies to act. In this they resemble Bourdieu's habitus: they are dispositions for action.

Even ideas can be explained by habits because ideas are – or originally have been – habits whose overt expression has been denied or blocked (Dewey 1922, 53). These situations of truncated habits tend to arouse images of previous encounters with similar problems and their possible solutions. Thus, thought and mental phenomena in general are treated as functional components of action by pragmatism: they "arise" in order to solve problematic action situations. However, habits constitute a phase in action processes. The concept of habit may bring to mind the analogy of an ecological niche. Ecological niches are the results of an organism adapting to its objective environment through gradual evolution. There is, however, the difference that habits are acquired rather than innate dispositions; they are units by which culture is inherited. The same goes for Bourdieu's habitus: it is "society written into the body, into the biological individual" (Bourdieu 1990b, 63). This does not mean that our natural proclivities are opposed to acquired ones, but there is still a conceptual difference between these forms of inheritance.[39]

Nevertheless, habits can never adapt to an environment (or environments) entirely, and therefore there is always the chance of conflict between a habit and its "habitat." This gives us the opportunity to distance ourselves from our habits and thus from the social circumstances that we happen to inhabit. Bourdieu (1990a, 56) argued that "*habitus* is a spontaneity without consciousness or will," but habits need not be opposed to will in such a manner. Habits constitute our selves and they *are* our will since they have projective power. In contemporary terminology, we can say that sensomotoric proclivities are a necessary basis even for our thought processes, abstract ones included, as the latter utilize, for example, different bodily metaphors (Lakoff & Johnson 1999). Thus, neither reason nor perception is free from the influence of habits, because both are vehicles for action and only make sense as part of action processes. Habits are also the unifying factor behind individual acts, as they are generalizations from particular responses. This means that what we call character is an interpenetration of different habits. Instead of character, one could also say that the interpenetration of different habits is what Bourdieu's habitus captures so well: habitus consists of all those different habits that situate us in our social spaces. However, habitus is not always necessarily related to a field or fields. For example, blue collar

---

[39] Pragmatists are usually more interested in the interplay between our natural and acquired proclivities than Bourdieusians. Such an interest does not mean that all of us should become biologists. However, one should leave the door open for the study of the way in which natural and acquired proclivities interact with each other.

workers are usually not interested in highbrow culture and therefore have no stakes in the actual cultural field. Thus, their habitus is not related to the cultural field. However, even if Bourdieusians do not always relate habitus to fields, their natural focus is always in cases where habitus is related to socioeconomic factors.

One must remember that "since environments overlap, since situations are continuous and those remote from one another contain like elements, a continuous modification of habits by one another is constantly going on" (Dewey 1922, 38). It is possible to achieve an integration of various habits, at least in principle, but it is in no way self-evident. This reconciliation of different action processes is an ongoing process, rather like Mead's (1967) generalized other, which indicates the possibility of integrating the attitudes of others into a more or less unified selfhood through the processes of identifying and distinguishing oneself from others (a theme discussed in the last section of the article). To state the matter differently, one's habitus can be related to a unified selfhood but if one's habits are related to very different fields, for example, then tensions are bound to ensue. Of course there can also exist a homology between these kinds of habits. For example, a writer can sell many books and thus develop a keen interest in financial matters (e.g., by investing his or her wealth). In this case there exists a homology between habits in the cultural and economic fields. However, such a homology often is *not* the case in reality; if a writer develops a too keen interest in money, he or she can eventually end up losing some of his or her cultural capital.

Habits and their overt manifestations are often mixed with each other. However, such alignment is problematic because in that case, as Hodgson (2006) reminds us, we would have to think that habits always cease to exist if no overt activity is visible. This implication would amount to a denial of the continuity of action which would be antithetical to the idea of habits. Thus, attitudes or dispositions to act in a specific fashion convey the idea of habits – and the idea behind habitus as well. It is commonplace to treat habit as a synonym for routines. However, this is not quite what Dewey or the other classical pragmatists had in mind, as Dewey explains here: "Repetition is in no sense the essence of habit. Tendency to repeat acts is an incident of many habits but not of all. ... The essence of habit is an acquired predisposition to *ways* or modes of response, not to particular acts except as, under special conditions, these express a way of behaving" (ibid., 42). Habits are thus general "policy recommendations" rather than individual acts (cf. Joas & Kilpinen 2006). In this they come very close to the idea behind habitus if habitus indicates a lifestyle.

In reading Dewey, one gets the impression that he sometimes overlooks this aspect of anticipating the possibilities for action, since he tends to emphasize the need for habit-change only when habits are already facing acute problems. However, anticipating problems certainly is a central part of our thought processes. Also in situations of current action problems, the failure of habits does not automatically and mechanically lead to novel solutions. Rather, this process is always mediated through images of the future consequences of possible scenarios. At any moment, the attempted resolution can also fail.

The pragmatist description of action does not deny reflexivity its important role, but it relegates it to a *phase* of action, albeit a very important one. To use the concepts proposed by Elder-Vass (2007, 341), one can distinguish a decision-taking phase and an action-implementing phase. Reflexivity is especially, if not exclusively, related to the former phase, and thus it is not needed at all times. However, I would hasten to add that even this decision-taking phase is a process of action, not something external to it. Therefore, both of these phases are, strictly speaking, action-implementing.[40] Reflexivity and habituality do not constitute a dichotomy in which the presence of the one necessarily precludes the other. Traditional behaviorism tends to reproduce the Cartesian dichotomy of thought and action because it focuses exclusively on action and thus presents us with "a monism of action" (Joas 1993, 71). To repeat myself, I want to emphasize that this exclusive focus on action, which can be found in behaviorism, is not what pragmatists are after. Mental phenomena undoubtedly do exist, and pragmatism explains them as related to a crisis in whatever we happen to be doing (broadly construed). Bourdieu (1990a, 61) also developed this idea as well when he argued that "the *habitus* tends to protect itself from crises and critical challenges by providing itself with a milieu to which it is as pre-adapted as possible." Thus we also actively seek particular environments to which our habits are well-suited rather than just wait passively for crises of action to mold our habits.

The term "crisis" can lead one to think only of major turning points in life or major societal changes (such as wars). Naturally, these major events are included in the category of a crisis, but action also encounters obstacles in our daily life that are much more mundane. These obstacles can involve, for example, disagreements with other actors and ensuing negotiations with them. Crises are often mundane and also plentiful. If nothing else changes, then our "inner environment" poses challenges for us, for example, through the aging of our bodies. Therefore, conflicts between habits and their environments are always more or less present, owing to the multiple stimuli that we encounter. These stimuli are not only environmental, but they also originate in the associations that our minds formulate all the time. In general, one can say that our mind "*monitors* or *supervises* the ongoing action process, and it *reconstructs* that process if it fails" (Joas & Kilpinen 2006, 325).

---

40 As Joas (1993: 71) explains, pragmatism argues against "the false Cartesian alternative of action as purely physical movement versus thought as purely mental construct."

Points of Contention: Creativity and Identity

Bourdieu and pragmatism undoubtedly share a critical attitude towards a divorce of theory and practice, or "intellectualism," as Bourdieu called it. Instead of an intellectualistic attitude, they emphasize the way in which practice is central to our societal being. However, there are also major differences between Bourdieu and classical pragmatists. These differences have to do with the way in which they stress the role of creativity (or the lack of it) and with their societal conceptions.

I will first deal with the issue of creativity. In his well known book, Hans Joas (1996) argues that pragmatism is a theory of situated creativity. One could say that creativity does not percolate "from above." Rather, it is situated in our concrete action situations. I already mentioned that habits are acquired rather than innate. This means that they are influenced by prior activities. Thus, even when one is faced with new situations one tends to respond in relation to old habits. These old habits are thus used as a point of comparison. This is not to deny an element of creativity. However, it is patterned creativity at the most. This means that radical novelty is almost impossible. As Noë (2009) argues, if we were to stumble upon such radical novelty, we would probably have a hard time in discerning anything of value in it. This is a point that both pragmatists and Bourdieusians would accept. For example, Bourdieu argues that there are instances of mismatch between our habitus and field(s) and only these instances are places for serious doubt and questioning. Thus, creativity is anchored in those situations in which it is encountered in. However, pragmatism is more centered on a theory of action than Bourdieu ever was and therefore pragmatists also discus this issue at length. This can give the impression that pragmatists emphasize the role of creativity more than Bourdieu.

As mentioned, Aboulafia (1999, 156) has made an important point in arguing that "Mead's "me" is comparable to Bourdieu's *habitus*." However, rather than conflating habits and habitus, I would argue that habitus is comprised of such particular habits that are related to socioeconomic factors. Mead's "me" consists of habits and is not quite the same thing as habitus. The "me" is often the conservative side of action, reproducing social structures, and highlighting this facet has led to accusations that reflexivity is lacking in Mead's thought (Archer 2007, 2003). These critiques are ill-founded in the case of Mead (Gronow 2008a); in relation to Bourdieu one can argue, as, for example, Sweetman (2003) and Brubaker (1993) do, that it is possible to develop a reflexive habitus. This possibility is something that Bourdieu himself also hints at when he discusses the possibility of socio-analysis, that is, looking at one's social background and its effects on one's views. It is more likely that changing social environments arouse more reflexivity than stable ones. Even though habits are mostly conservative, we should remember that there is always the problem of intertwining habits, mentioned by Dewey. Bourdieu relates this problem of "intertwining" with social differentiation because the development of relatively autonomous social worlds, that is, fields, gives more liberty to "complex strategies of the habitus" (Bourdieu 1990b, 73). Therefore, the integration of habits is by no means self-evident, and this factor is bound to lead to crises, which call for reflexive deliberation. These crises can also be anticipated in advance by cultivating reflexive habits. This cultivation does not mean mere individual practice but the way in which, for example, our educational institutions can foster such reflexivity.

One could argue that science is an institution that is dedicated to this sort of anticipation of possible crises of habits. This is not to say that science would always take a reflexive stance towards its own practices. However, Dewey thought that – rightly understood – science and education can foster a healthy reflexivity, and thus creativity, towards social habits. Bourdieu was more skeptical about the reflexivity enhancing potential of these institutions. He was even critical of such reflexivity because it can lead to an intellectualistic attitude which divorces theory from practice. However, turning reflexivity towards itself is a project that Bourdieu embraces. According to him, only the science of sociology, as an instrument of socio-analysis, can free us from the baggage of our habitus.

In Mead's work, in addition to the "me" (the internalized attitudes of others), we find its conceptual counterpart, the "I." This concept refers to the impulsive side of action and of our selves. There is no equivalent to the "I" in Bourdieu's work. The "I" is the impulsive response of the individual to the habitual and social attitudes one encounters. This response is always "more or less uncertain" (Mead 1967, 176), and, in its turn, it can change those social attitudes. According to Dewey, impulses are "the pivots upon which the re-organization of activities turn, they are agencies of deviation, for giving new directions to old habits and changing their quality" (Dewey 1922, 93). However, these impulses are flexible since their complex *interaction* with the social environment (Mead's "me") and with other impulses is what counts. The presence of the "I" in Mead's work and the role of impulses in Dewey's thought give us a more active picture of agency than the one Bourdieu presents.

In this scheme of things, intelligent thought is "of the nature of inhibitive selection" (Veblen 1919, 6). Reflexive thought inhibits us from following all the possible impulses and suggestions that happen to spring to mind. Our impulses and our intelligence can, and often do, join forces, rather than opposing each other: through training we can make the process of inhibitive selection of impulses more or less habitual. When habituality becomes a dead routine, free of reflection, or even hostile towards reflection, then the sort of domination that Bourdieu underscores easily becomes the norm. Elder-Vass (2007, 329) has argued that "there is confusion about the apparent conflict between Bourdieu's stress on the subconscious operation of habitus and his heavily qualified acceptance of some role for conscious thought." This argument is perhaps not quite fair towards Bourdieu. Nevertheless, it seems clear to me that pragmatists focus much more on this issue of creative activity than Bourdieu. Thus, this is a major difference of emphasis.

Dewey's ideal was a form of reflexive habituality in which an actor is able to adapt and change his or her habits of need be instead of clinging to them (possibly until the bitter end). There are no general guidelines as to when habits have outlived their environments. Rather, habits have to be assessed on a case by case basis. A habit is not a conservative element as such: "whether an ability is limited to repetition of past acts adopted to past conditions or is available for new emergencies depends wholly upon what *kind* of habit exists" (Dewey 1922, 66, emphasis added). There are then different kinds of habits, and enslaving oneself to old ruts leads to conservative results, but this is not the whole meaning of habits. The problem with this sort of enslavement is that it fails to master "the conditions which *now* enter into action" (ibid., 67). There are also lessons to be drawn for social and political discussions. Dewey preferred gradual reforms to revolutionary ideologies. Revolutionary ideologies usually presume that they can do away with people's habits for good or they do not even conceptualize the habitual dimension. It is possible to think that mere legal reform will change society. Naturally, it often does but the existence of habits also should be taken into account. Trying to change all habits at once is practically impossible and bound to lead to individual or social suffering.

Dewey might have been a bit too optimistic about the extent of which people are capable of assessing the validity of their habits. When one compares this vision with Bourdieu's views, it becomes apparent that Bourdieu is more critical of the role of reforms and the extent of social reflexivity people are capable of achieving. For example, the logic of fields as sites of struggle seems to preclude genuine co-operation. More importantly, even a reflexive attitude can be interpreted as stake in a symbolic struggle for domination. Our dispositions, embodied in the habitus and taking the form of different social and cultural capitals, are "acquired through learning processes associated with protracted dealings with the regularities of the field [in question]" (Bourdieu 2005, 8-9). By way of definition, Bourdieu said, for example, that a field is "a network, or a configuration, of objective relations between positions" (Bourdieu & Wacquant 1992, 97). These positions are occasions for struggles for the particular capital accumulated in the fields. In short, the amount of capital one has determines one's position in a field, and power tends to accumulate in certain positions. In addition, there often is a homology between positions in different fields. Thus, a particular position in, say, the cultural field can also indicate a comparable position in some other field. The limits of fields are defined by the types of capital characteristic of them. For example, in the scientific field, it is scientific authority or competence that one struggles for and that defines one's position. The picture Bourdieu paints is therefore one of relentless competition and struggle over hierarchical social positions.

Mead's pragmatism differs from Bourdieu in that it has a notion of the so-called generalized other. This concept does not refer to particular "others" but to generalizations that we have made based on the attitudes of others. The ability to take the attitudes of other, so to speak, is what enables self-reflection in the first place. Thus, sociality and individuality are in no way opposed to each other but rather mutually constitutive. Mead (1967, 265) argued that "until one can respond to himself as the community responds to him, he does not genuinely belong to the community." Thus, what makes us humans truly social is our ability to take the attitudes of other towards ourselves. This attitude taking happens gradually through a development process where we learn that other people exhibit certain attitudes towards our different lines of conduct. By taking these attitudes one can anticipate the possible reactions of others. Thus, one regards oneself as an object, that is, becomes self-conscious by identifying with the attitudes of others. However, only in childhood do we anticipate the reactions of concrete others, those of our parents in particular. Later on in life, we tend to take the attitudes of more abstract others, for example, people in our age group or other people living in our country.

These generalized attitudes – which Mead called the generalized other – towards ourselves and towards our surroundings can at first sight seem oppressive. However, the more general one's other, the more one can reflect on the particular social environment that happens to be one's lot. Thus, relativism and the oppression of individuality are a problem if one limits oneself to particular social environments and particular perspectives, not if one generalizes one's perspective and possible reactions with the help of more general social attitudes. Sociality is actually a precondition for self-reflection and for social change. Mead's ideal was a sort of a universal generalized other; even the possibility of taking the attitudes of the whole of humanity. Thus, we are discussing a process of identifying with others rather than a process of making distinctions. Whether such a universal generalized other is possible or not, it is clear that Meadian sociality differs from Bourdieu. The picture Bourdieu paints is one of constant social conflict between and within fields. Usually social reproduction does its trick so well that no open conflicts are present but in Bourdieu's conception social identity is all about differentiating oneself from others.

How would it be possible to cultivate more and more "generalized others?" Mead did not really ponder on this issue but John Dewey has an answer (although Dewey did not use Meadian vocabulary): through education and public discussion. Education should not be about brainwashing the minds of the youth but about fostering a critical attitude towards social habits. In addition, Dewey believed that the role of the public is essential in a democratic society. Rather than being a field of its own in Bourdieu's sense of the term, the public is open to all concerns. How are those concerns to be communicated there? Through fostering a critical, scientific, method towards social issues. For Dewey, this does not indicate an attitude of non-democratic social engineering but rather being able to look at the consequences of beliefs that concern social issues. Social and even moral issues should not be left at the mercy of arbitrary authority, for example. The need to control the consequences of social action arises almost in itself but social movements are the key if these consequences are to be made public. Thus, social movements are a factor in social change. All in all, the Meadian and Deweyan picture of society is much more democratic than Bourdieu's vision. His vision is a critical theory that unmasks the domination that misrecognition conceals: the arbitrariness that is implied by the correlation between social positions and our dispositions. However, a Deweyan would argue that unmasking this domination is possible only through educational and public reforms.

Where Does this Leave Us?

For Bourdieu, classifications and other ways of thinking that may seem natural to us are in reality the results of historical processes. However, this historicism does not lead to a relativist nihilism or despair. Bourdieu (1990a, 25) argued, for example, that "[i]t is in discovering its historicity that reason gives itself the means of escaping from history." Thus, it is possible to reflect on one's categories of thinking by situating these categories in their historical context. I fully agree that precisely such an operation is one of the basic tasks of sociology. Pragmatists also argue for the importance of reflexivity but Bourdieu states more explicitly the social preconditions of reflexivity. However, despite the best of intentions, such a historical reflection can lead to a "protorelativistic" attitude: if our beliefs vary according to time and place, why should anyone care enough to be reflexive about one's beliefs? Pragmatists would recognize the importance of being reflexive but, besides reflexivity, they would promote also another principle, namely, the principle of fallibilism. Fallibilism states that a major way in which we learn anything is by learning from our mistakes. Therefore one can never be sure that one's beliefs are correct but this is not a reason for despair or skepticism. What this situation calls for is a readiness to change our beliefs if need be. Well, how can one know when to change one's beliefs? Not through general guidelines but by being self-reflexive in the way that Bourdieu advocates: in the case of science, by being aware of one's position in the scientific field and on the possible implications that this position can have on one's research. Thus, fallibilism and reflexivity should go hand in hand if one wants to continue the research agenda outlined by Bourdieu.

The point of this article has been to show that Bourdieu and pragmatism share many concerns but that they also paint somewhat different pictures of societal relations. They approach society with somewhat different concerns in mind: for Bourdieu, structural reproduction is the key whereas for pragmatists (and especially for Mead), issues of sociality are the starting point. Thus, it could be argued that they approach societal phenomena from different sides. Is it possible to relate these conceptions to each other? I would argue that to some existent this is possible and also even feasible.

A recurring theme in Bourdieu's reception has been the charge that he reduces action to mere status aspirations (e.g., Archer 2007). In reality, Bourdieu himself was not guilty of such a reduction. It has often escaped the attention of his commentators that his ideas mainly pertain to phenomena on the population level. Bourdieu posits statistical correlations between dispositions and positions and these correlations do not say anything about particular cases. Thus, one's socioeconomic background does not directly determine anything but, on the level of the population, it can be seen as predisposing people with different social backgrounds to favor certain tastes, for example. However, the logic of the fields and the associated struggle is a schema that should be applied with some caution. Social structures are not always points of struggle and neither is action, even habitual action, necessarily explicitly related to socioeconomic differences. Or to state the matter differently, habitual action, which is a (or even *the*) building block of social structures, does not correlate with socioeconomic status in every case. One could even argue that habitus is a special case of habits. It refers to those habits that are related to our socioeconomic background and to our present status – to those dispositions that correlate with our position in a field. In some cases, habitus is a systematic combination of socioeconomic and field-related habits. Habitual reactions can be present without a systematic habitus, that is, without a socioeconomic lifestyle as an indicator of certain kinds of symbolic capital. This means that habits are not the same thing as a habitus and the former cannot be replaced with the latter.

A counterargument would say that it is only a matter of nitpicking to compare Bourdieu's concept of habitus or the habit-concept of pragmatists. Even if there are differences in these conceptions, do these differences have any implications for concrete sociological research? And even if there would be some possible implications for sociological research, power relations are surely the bread and butter of sociology. These arguments are to the point but only to an extent. If we agree on the centrality of power relations and on the relevance of socioeconomic factors for these relations, then we can admit that it is Bourdieu that always gets the upper hand in comparison with the pragmatists. However, I do not think that a focus on power relations necessarily excludes other issues from our sociological research agenda. Here is an example that hopefully shows that the difference between the concepts of habitus and habit might have some implications for the way in which we interpret empirical results: A study by Nihtilä and Martikainen (2008) argues that the elderly have a higher risk of being admitted to institutional care after the death of one's spouse. That is, if your spouse happens to die (and you are in the age group 65 or older), there is a good chance that you will not make it on your own. What makes this – admittedly somewhat unsurprising – result interesting is that "the overall effect of bereavement did not significantly vary according to the level of income or education" (ibid., 1231). Usually health issues vary according to socioeconomic variables but this case is an exception.

Nihtilä and Martikainen (ibid., 1232) offer various explanations for the excess risk of admission to institutional care following the death of a spouse: the loss of social and instrumental support, emotional stress and physical diseases caused by stress and grief. These explanations may all be credible but it is also possible to argue that they are all related to one thing: a crisis in habits. A major part of the environment of our action, and therefore a major part of our habits, has to do with other people. Take away a spouse, a very emotional relationship to one's environment, and some sort of a crisis is bound to ensue. In this case, the environment of action changes so much that many elderly find it impossible to learn those new habits that would enable them to cope with this dramatic change.

Here we have, then, an empirical case that begs for a sociological explanation – it is, after all, a change in social circumstances that is taking place – and one that cannot be explained with the help of socioeconomic factors, at least in the case of the Finnish elderly.[41] Even if it were so that Bourdieu's concept of habitus is not always related to a distinct field (or fields), I would argue that in this empirical case the concept of habit is more appropriate for our purposes. One's socioeconomic standing is not related to the risk of being admitted to institutional care and, in my reading, habitus is a concept that is especially well suited to those cases where there is a strong interaction with socioeconomic variables and the issue under investigation. Therefore my interpretation of this case says that a crisis of habits takes place and some are, fortunately, able to cope with the situation by reconstructing their habits. This can be seen in the fact that the risk of not making it on your own is highest during the first month after the death of one's spouse and it decreases with time. The excess risk is also related to gender because it is much higher for men. This finding should come as no surprise since men are more reliant on their spouses in their household habits (especially in the older generations).[42]

Naturally, many, if not most, of our habits are related to aspects of our socioeconomic background but we can treat this question as an empirical rather than as a conceptual issue. In other words, which habits are elements of fields – and in what manner – does not have to be settled *a priori*. With Bourdieu's work, we can also supplement pragmatism with a description of the way in which our socioeconomic background is often a part of our doings. As Colapietro (2004, 79) argues, "relations of power are stressed and examined by Bourdieu in ways useful for anyone desirous to carry forward the deeper aspirations of Deweyan pragmatism." These aspirations in-

---

41 As Nihtilä and Martikainen (2008, 1232-1233) argue, the situation might be different in countries where publicly provided institutional care is not equally accessible regardless of income.
42 This finding could, of course, initiate Bourdieusian interpretations having to do with the way in which division of labor is based on gender. However, this is an issue that cannot be discussed here.

clude the idea that when the habitual reproduction of social structures becomes merely routine, power relations can easily disadvantage (some) actors. However, habitual action does not necessarily imply sticking to "mindless" routine. Some habits are always needed, since they are the basis on which we can consider other possible habits. The potential for monopolizing social thinking is a real problem in all modern societies with extensive divisions of labor. Bourdieu can help us in formulating the dangers resulting from this problem (e.g., the reproduction of inter-generational socioeconomic positions and related dispositions). Bourdieu also points out that reflection should reflect on itself if it is to be genuine reflection.

Social identity is about making distinctions, that is, about what one is *not*. However, a big part of social identity is about identifying with others. Mead's ideal was a universal generalized other and the possibility of taking the attitudes of the whole of humanity. Thus, in his thought one can also identify with those who do not share our socioeconomic habits (i.e., our habitus). This can sound a bit naïve to the ears of Bourdieusians. In addition, one could criticize Mead for assuming that social differentiation somehow automatically brings about an awareness of mutual dependence. Even if it would bring about such awareness, a Bourdieusian can argue that this awareness can act as an obstacle on the way towards genuine equality – if this awareness only acts as a vehicle for making distinctions. Thus, being aware of my place in socially differentiated positions can act as a legitimation for existing social hierarchies. However, Mead's generalized other points out that sociality is not just about making distinctions in a hierarchical order. It is also, maybe even on a more fundamental level, about *identifying* with others and with their reactions towards us and our social world. Sociality is thus twofold: who one is and who one is not. As Sen (2010, 353) has argued, generalizing from particular perspectives can lead to recognition of multiple and over-lapping identities which act as a remedy for sectarian demagogy.

Bourdieu explained that he "said habitus so as *not* to say habit" (Bourdieu & Wacquant 1992, 122). However, he was referring to the habit-concept in its traditional meaning as mere routine. Pragmatists also acknowledge that there are routines but this is not the only meaning that the term "habit" has in their hands. Therefore one should have both habitus *and* habit in one's conceptual arsenal.

CHAPTER 5

Integrating the Capabilities Approach with Pragmatism[43]

When one consults political analyses of societal development made by economists, one usually finds that development is identified with economic development or, more specifically, with economic growth. The means of measuring economic development differ to some extent, but the most common form of measurement is the Gross National Product (GNP) of nations. Its problems are well known. It does not, for example, take into account how wealth is distributed across populations. The most important question is whether development is the same thing as economic growth or should growth be seen as only a means to more substantial forms of social development. These questions have been at the forefront of Amartya Sen's developmental economics. Sen has become famous as a representative of the capabilities approach, which stresses actual positive freedoms instead of mere negative freedom (the lack of constraints). According to this approach, the worth of economic development is to be evaluated against a backdrop of more substantial criteria that have to do with freedom of action. Martha C. Nussbaum is another representative of the capabilities approach, which has, all in all, drawn a considerable amount of attention (see, e.g., the volume edited by Nussbaum and Sen 1993).

The capability approach presents some interesting ideas that are useful in assessing social development and social reforms. However, this approach also raises important and age-old questions having to do with action, societal change and the relation of the individual to society. Sen himself notices the presence of these issues, at least in passing. He wants to reserve an active role for the targets of reforms. While doing this, he resorts to arguments that emphasize the value-laden nature of action (instead of seeing actors as maximizers of utility). This is a move in the right direction, but referring to values is insufficient if the underlying theory of action remains unchanged.

[43] This chapter was originally published in Sami Pihlström & Henrik Rydenfelt (eds.): *Pragmatist Perspectives*. Acta Philosophica Fennica Vol. 86, 197-210.

Neither Sen nor Nussbaum discuss the fundamentals of action theory, and this is what I propose to do with the help of the pragmatist philosophy of action.

When discussing developmental issues, one also confronts the problem of relativism. According to Sen, even so-called authoritarian countries in the east have always had an interest in freedom of action. Even though it is important to note that freedom is not restricted to Western countries, Sen is not altogether free of the dangers of relativism. Therefore the capability approach needs to build a theoretical case for the intrinsic importance of freedom. Such an argument – and a complementary one to Sen's views – can be found in pragmatism. Pragmatism also helps in understanding why it is possible to argue, as Sen does, that freedom is a social product: it is dependent on social attitudes and it gets articulated in the public. The worth of freedom, however, is not a relative issue because it is an intrinsic feature of our intersubjective constitution.

The relevance of pragmatism for the capabilities approach has been suggested before. Zimmermann (2006) has argued that "turning back to pragmatism (…) will allow the development of a sociological and critical understanding of the capability approach." However, I argue that pragmatism allows us to approach "meta-sociological" issues related to capabilities rather than substantial sociological questions. Both the capability approach and pragmatism are part of the tradition of liberal thought, but they both have critical relations to liberalism. Here is their strength – and their "family resemblance." As Richard Bernstein (1987, 560) argues, "[t]he pragmatic legacy (…) will only be recovered and revitalized when we try to do for our time what Dewey did in his historical context – to articulate, texture and *justify* a vision of a pragmatically viable ideal of communal democracy." This is what I propose to do by relating pragmatism to the capabilities approach.

Beyond the GNP: Capabilities and Freedom

According to Sen (2001, 3), the "[g]rowth of GNP or of individual incomes can (…) be very important as *means* to expanding freedoms enjoyed by the members of society." Economic development should, then, be assessed as a means to other objectives – namely, freedom – rather than seen as an end in itself. Income and wealth are only "general-purpose means" that enable different freedoms. The economic situation is, of course, not the only determinant of freedoms, as social and other arrangements have their say in the matter. Sen's point is that the economistic model does not tell us enough about how people are able to live their lives. Unlike many economists that are individualists by profession, Sen argues that freedom is a social product. This is because social arrangements can – and should – expand individual freedoms. Freedom has a double role: it is both the end and also the primary means of development. Sen calls these aspects the constitutive and instrumental roles of freedom (ibid., 36). The constitutive role is related to substantive freedoms which include "elementary capabilities like being able to avoid such deprivations as starvation, undernourishment (…) as well as the freedoms that are associated with being literate and numerate, enjoying political participation and uncensored speech and so on" (ibid.).

Sen's exact definition for capabilities goes like this: "The *capability* of a person reflects the alternative combinations of functionings the person can achieve, and from which he or she can choose one collection" (Sen 1993, 31). These functionings can either be elementary ones, such as adequate nourishment, or more complex ones, as in "achieving self-respect or being socially integrated" (ibid.). Choosing a collection of functionings may sound a bit too much like rational choice theory, but the basic idea of not forcing functionings on anyone is a premise shared by all liberalist social philosophies. Sen does not want to present an extensive list of what these capabilities might be because they differ from one individual to another and they are also dependent on the wider social context. For example, in developing countries one "may be able to go a fairly long distance with a relatively small number of centrally important functionings and the corresponding basic capabilities" (ibid.). In better-off contexts, the list can be much longer and also more diverse. Thus the primary focus should be on the freedom to achieve valuable things rather than on achievement as such (Robeyns 2005). This is not too revolutionary an idea because it amounts to giving equal opportunities to all independently of their origin of birth. As a developmental economist, Sen is alert to the lack of realization of this idea for the bulk of humanity.

Capabilities, then, refer to *the actual abilities* that people have to achieve certain things that are part of the well-being of society. The task of the capability approach is to evaluate to what extent these abilities are realized or, in other words, to evaluate the alternative capability sets people have (these being the real *opportunities*). These criteria are used as the informational basis of evaluation – what is considered as relevant information in assessing social development – rather than focusing exclusively on utility or liberty, as other social philosophies have done (Sen 1985). The context of Sen's developmental economics, as that of developmental economics in general, is usually confined to so-called developing countries. However, there is no reason why we should limit its application in this manner. The capability approach can be used as an informational basis in evaluating social reforms *in general*. Our goal can be one of enhancing the relevant options available, while also keeping in mind the influence of existing habits on the capability sets that people are actually able to put to use.

Actors: Passive and Active

Sen (2001, 137) argues that his capability approach goes hand in hand with emphasizing the importance of agency, as "seeing people as agents rather than as patients." People should not, then, be treated as mere passive recipients of social reforms. When discussing action, Sen departs from the common economistic mold and argues that self-interest is not the only motivating factor behind action. It is hard to disagree with Sen on this matter – but even Sen does not spell out what is really at stake here. As Sen argues, there certainly are values and norms operating in capitalistic economies, and therefore self-interest is not the only, or even the primary, motivating factor. However, for a sociological audience this sounds all too familiar, because Talcott Parsons proposed a similar idea in his famous book *The Structure of Social Action* (1937). Parsons worried that the so-called rational action theories of economists are not able to explain why people act cooperatively. This is a problem for all theories that try to explain action from individualistic premises. He argued that the normative and value consensus of society directs individual actors towards common goals.

However, the stress on societal values eventually led Parsons to see values independently of action. Analyzing values can thus lead one to see actors as mere passive recipients and puppets directed by values, if the underlying theory of action remains passive. If Sen wants to be free of seeing people as passive "patients," he should follow different lines of thinking, because referring to values does not guarantee an active position for actors. This point was eventually made in critiques directed at Parsonian thinking within social theory. One reaction was to emphasize the knowledgeability of actors (Giddens 1986), and the social construction of this knowledge (Berger & Luckmann 1966). An unhappy consequence of this critique is that in many cases it led, in its turn, into studying knowledge and conceptions of action at the expense of action and independently of it. This paved the way for yet another passive view of actors, one that portrays actors as mere containers of social knowledge (Gronow 2008b, 359-360).

Things are not, however, as sad as my lamenting might lead one to conclude. There is a viable option for both normative theories of action and for the social constructionism camp, and this option is pragmatism. Pragmatism consistently stresses the importance of action: action does not need any motivation because it is something that happens anyway (Kilpinen 2000; 2008b). According to pragmatists, it is a "utilitarian fallacy" – shared by many economists in particular – to discuss actors as passive instances that always need negative or positive cues to move them about. What makes it utilitarian is the similarity with the basic premise of utilitarian philosophy, which argues for the importance of looking at negative and positive consequences. As a premise of social philosophy, it is worthwhile to alleviate the sufferings of people (attending to negative consequences of social action), but it is a different thing to argue that people would always need positive or negative reinforcements for any action to take place (see Mead 1936). This important distinction has often gone unnoticed in utilitarian thinking.

In order to avoid seeing people as passive patients, one is well advised – as a general rule – to focus on what people are *doing* instead of focusing on their possible motives. The narrow focus on mere motives usually leads one to analyze individual actions. This is problematic because these individual acts are always parts of larger action processes. For example, social reforms affect people that are always already in action. Thus one should analyze how these reforms affect ongoing action processes. Different social reforms often tend to destabilize existing habits. There is nothing wrong with crisis situations as such (i.e., destabilized habits), but if reforms are of such magnitude that they affect *all or many* of the habit sets of the parties involved, then problems are bound to ensue. The ideal situation of change for pragmatist philosophers is therefore gradual reform instead of total revolution. This enables one to assess the impact of reforms against the background of stable habits. The extra-discursive capacities embedded in habits deserve attention because they reveal the embodied interactions sustaining our "life-world" (Lyng & Franks 2002, 177).

Revolutionary ideologies – and often practical policies as well – tend to forget the force of existing habits and the fact that change does not come about through mere legal reform, or even through stressing new values. Legal rules as well as values are always grounded in habits which do not change as easily as explicit rules and such. However, habits are not just a nuisance on the way to reforms. Rather, they are rationalities of action that deserve to be heard through public discussion. Only those habits should be deemed irrational which are opposed to reflexive thought *per se* and are therefore in principle incapable of revision through reason. Old habits die hard, but they need to be revised as we meet new and changing environments of action. The remaking of old habits "through the union with the new is precisely what intelligence is" (Dewey 2000, 56).

The Issue of Relativism

Now it is time to move on to the other part of my main argument, that is, why Sen could benefit from pragmatism in discussing the problem of cultural relativism. In brief, it is because "he has never produced explicit arguments against relativism, apart from historical arguments" (Nussbaum 2000, 13). Sen endorses the view that freedom is a social product. This does not mean that he is a relativist because he also discusses at length the so-called cultural critique which asks the very fundamental question of whether there are any ethics that could be called universal. And if not, whether this means that our values have no legitimate validity claims outside the cultural sphere in which they belong to. Sen focuses on the arguments of the advocates of "Asian values" who attack the notion of universal values on the basis of the supposed authoritarianism of Asia (Sen 2001, 231). Against relativism, he goes to pains to show that in Asia "[t]here are no quintessential values that apply to this immensely large and heterogeneous population," at least "none that separate them out as a group from people in the rest of the world" (ibid.). If we look closely enough, we will find both authoritarian features in the history of the West and the highlighting of the value of freedom in Asian thought as well. So freedom and, as a consequence, the domain of capabilities are of potential interest in every culture because elements related to freedom are present in very diverse cultural settings. However, besides this relevant argument, we can also argue that this potential interest in freedom and capabilities is due to the constitution of human beings as self-reflexive actors. This argument differs from Sen's because if it is accepted, then we do not have to search for the particular manifestations of freedom in every culture (however interesting this search might be in itself).

I already mentioned that freedom is for Sen a social product; that is, it is dependent on social arrangements and therefore "[t]here is a deep complementarity between individual agency and social arrangements" (Sen 2001, xii). John Dewey (2000, 42) also argues that "effective liberty is a function of the social conditions existing at any time." Both Sen and Dewey, then, highlight the fact that mere negative freedom (the absence of formal constraints) does not automatically entail greater freedom of action. For Dewey, the neglect of this insight is the reason for the failure of liberalism to fulfill its promise as a social philosophy. From Mead we can get conceptual means into the interdependence of freedom and the social context. Mead can be of help because his theory portrays a social picture of the *self*. So much so that Mead has been interpreted as arguing for a theory of selfhood completely dictated by its social environment (e.g., Archer 2003). As I argue elsewhere (Gronow 2008a), Mead does not profess to such a complete "social construction," even though he does claim that proper selfhood is born only after one is able to take the attitudes of others towards oneself. This taking of the attitudes of others is the developmental way through which we can become objects to ourselves – "seeing" ourselves through the eyes of others – and proper selfhood entails being an object to oneself.

The general situation that Mead (1967, 251) presents is as follows: "The community as such creates its environment by being sensitive to it." For every living form, the environment exists properly speaking in those selective and possible responses that the form in question has towards its surroundings. Therefore, "the meaning which our world has (...) lie[s] in what we are going to do with it" (Mead 1936, 90). It does not lie merely in what we know, in our typifications and knowledge schemas, as the standard social constructionist argument goes (see Berger & Luckmann 1966). Our attention is selective and tends to favor stimuli that relate to what we are doing. This is not a relativist argument; one could call this stance "relational" (cf. Lyng & Franks 2002). The centrality of doing things in the world is also the background for our knowledge-seeking activities. The human situation is a special case because due to the self-reflexive nature of our selves, analysis of our responses to our environments of action becomes possible before actually responding or reacting to them. From this basis, Mead (1967, 251) argues that "even those problems which come from within the community itself can be definitely controlled by the community." It follows that social control is essentially about *self-criticism*. So far even your everyday critical theorist might agree, but things get more complicated when we come to Mead's conclusion: "Hence social control, so far from tending to crush out the human individual or to obliterate his self-conscious individuality, is, on the contrary, actually constitutive of and inextricably associated with that of individuality" (Mead 1967, 255).

We become individuals only through our societal relations, through taking the generalized attitudes of others (this is what Mead called *the generalized other*). Therefore it can be argued that "[t]he society that we belong to gives us our peculiar selves" (Mead 1936, 101). However, society does not have any transcendental existence because it is comprised of acting human beings – ones that take the attitudes of others toward themselves (usually more or less habitually). This social process enables control of and over the environment of action. Other animals also encounter problematic situations as they act in their ever-changing environments. They have to adapt to these changes or they will simply perish. The human animal is exceptional because it can control its own environment through taking the attitude of the environment toward itself. Thus it is possible to adapt to environmental changes by consciously changing one's behavior. In addition, it is also possible to control these changes in the environment or even to instigate them intentionally in the first place. Thus, the birth of proper and reflexive selves and the ability to control one's environment are mutually constitutive processes. Of course one can never achieve total control over the environment (witness the issue of global warming); not even the institutional or cultural environment is transparent or malleable enough for us to control it as we please. However, there is a qualitative difference between merely *adjusting* to environmental changes and being able to *control* those changes.

Social integration is not, as such, in any way opposed to the individuality of those actors who comprise the social whole in question. Particular social institutions can, of course, oppress individuality, but institutions are not oppressive by definition. And what's even more important, "without social institutions of some sorts (...) there could be no fully mature individual selves or personalities" (ibid., 262). Liberalists have tended to see social arrangements as mere constraints on pre-existing individuality. However, if we recognize that individuality is not ready-made and already possessed, then removing legal and other formal restrictions is no guarantee for its blossoming, either (Dewey 2000, 46).

Now we are in a position where we can present constitutive reasons for Sen's argument on freedom being a social product. We can say that "until one can respond to himself as the community responds to him, he does not genuinely belong to the community" (Mead 1967, 265). Without such an attitude, there can be no proper, objective meaning, and no truly rational conduct either. Mead's social ideal was such that would involve a "universalized other," taking, at least in principle, the attitudes of a progressively wider community – that of humanity in universal communication. A fruitless relativism resulting from the encounter with different social arrangements does not present itself in Mead's scheme because selves are *always* dependent on taking the attitudes of a wider community. The wider the scope of one's community, the wider is one's freedom in assessing relevant action situations and in "escaping" from particular and *relative* social attitudes.

The existence of different social attitudes does not mean that one's own attitude is wholly arbitrary; it is not if it is based on taking into account the attitudes of a wider community. Not all attitudes are of course equally justifiable. It is indeed possible to assess social attitudes: they gain weight through being *open-minded* and *self-critical* because these are factors that enable this assessment in the first place. One should not, of course, be self-critical to such a degree that it paralyzes one's efforts. Habits are therefore always needed as a basis of action, but the ideal is a reflexive habit – the habit of changing habits according to situational demands. Our focus should be on the consequences of different social attitudes because these are the context for the formation of capabilities (cf. Robeyns 2005, 99). Generally speaking, those attitudes that further the capabilities and freedoms of actors are to be judged as best, and, accordingly, those that harm them are detrimental. But where is this judging of social attitudes to be done and who is to do it? Scientific inquiry is the *method* by which we can approach this issue (cf. Dewey 2000, 53). However, when it comes to capabilities, it is not only for scientific professionals to do the judging. Sen and the pragmatists agree that therefore the role of the public is essential in this process.

Capabilities and the Role of the Public

As already mentioned, Sen does not want to present us with an extensive list of capabilities. The absence of such a list, however, is an intentional move on his part, and it is Sen's aim to address these judgemental issues explicitly – the unsatisfactory alternative being "hiding them in some implicit framework" (Sen 2001, 75). However, for practical purposes one has to have some sort of consensus on what weights to give to particular issues. This is, according to Sen (ibid., 78-79), "a 'social choice' exercise, and it requires public discussion and a democratic understanding and acceptance." Therefore the conceptualization of people's needs and preferences is a factor that cannot be assessed without public discussion and open debates (ibid., 153).

However, Robeyns (2005, 106) has argued that in Sen's theory, "it is not at all clear how these processes of public reasoning and democracy are going to take place, and how we make sure that minimal conditions of fair representation are guaranteed." According to John Dewey's (1927) classical theory of the public, the public emerges – or at least it should emerge – when there are societal issues that affect "third parties." It is the *consequences* of social action that are in need of attention. This idea of judging social arrangements on the basis of their consequences can be dated back to Jeremy Bentham's liberalism (Dewey 2000, 26). The distinction between the private and the public therefore lies in the consequences of transactions. These can be twofold: "those which affect the persons directly engaged in a transaction and those which affect others beyond those immediately concerned" (Dewey 1927, 12). When there are consequences of the second type, we are in the realm of the public. However, not even all indirect consequences are deserving of the public's attention. Dewey has in mind those particular consequences that also "are so important as to need control, whether by inhibition or by promotion" (ibid., 15).

Dewey also gives more defining characteristics for the aforementioned consequences: their far-reaching character in space or time and "their settled, uniform and recurrent nature, and their irreparableness" (ibid., 64). There is no sharp line to be drawn between private matters and those that need public regulation, and therefore this line has to be discovered experimentally. Here we see Dewey's pragmatist credentials: he avoids erecting fundamental distinctions and favors experimentation in action instead (e.g., ibid., 202-203). Earlier on we saw that Sen is clearly committed to democratic ideals. We can also safely say that Dewey was a democrat if there ever was one (as is argued by Westbrook 1991, among others). Dewey (1927, 148) goes so far as to argue that if democracy is regarded as an idea, it is "not an alternative to other principles of associated life. It is the idea of community life itself." That is to say, democracy is inherent as an ideal in the very idea of a community. And furthermore: "The clear consciousness of a community life, with all its implications, constitutes the idea of democracy" (ibid., 149). Democracy is for Dewey an "opportunity for all citizens to achieve both 'self-realization' and positive fraternal association" (Whipple 2005, 161). Mere universal suffrage is not sufficient for the realization of this goal. In addition to the absence of constraints, it demands a social organization that encourages its existence.

Whipple argues that "Dewey's emphasis on democracy as an 'end' results from his social-psychological perspective" (ibid.). Mead had a similar, social-psychological, justification for the interdependence of individuality and social organization as Dewey here has for the value of democracy. Both arguments rest on a foundation where the realization of the self is possible only in social relations and, actually, is *due* to those very relations. Sen's thinking is not that far away from Mead and Dewey, either. In words that could be authored by Sen, Dewey (1927, 150) has the following to say: "Liberty is that secure release and fulfilment of personal potentialities which take place only in rich and manifold association with others: the power to be an individualized self making a distinctive contribution and enjoying in its own way the fruits of association." In other words, Deweyan democracy requires the ensuring of capabilities.

What the public does, in Dewey's scheme of things, is that it communicates the consequences of actions that affect it indirectly. Therefore there is at first a problematic situation which shakes the habitual foundations of action. Individual habits get into crises all the time, but the interesting cases are those that affect societal habits – common ways of acting in a particular context that often are not discursively articulated. However, not even all societal habits are the proper interest of the Deweyan public. For example, changing fashions can, and often do, disrupt societal habits but they usually are not directly related to capabilities. Those social attitudes that are related to capabilities need the public's help when their foundations are shaken. This is therefore the place of democratic agency. Naturally the state is an important actor in this regard, but social movements are a case in point, as well. Dewey's conception of the public does not coincide with what is often meant by the public sphere. The latter includes also conversation topics that are not important enough to need public regulation. Celebrity news, for example, is not usually related to important, indirect consequences of action in Dewey's sense, even though it is a part of the public *sphere*.

Conclusion

According to Dewey's criterion of the public, capability issues clearly belong to the public domain. Indeed, it seems useful to unite the arguments of both Sen and the pragmatists because this offers theoretical depth for Sen in other issues as well. Thus we have an active view of agency, a social view of freedom and an explanation for the role of the public. In addition, this discussion opens the way for a contemporary formulation of the social philosophical issues of pragmatism. Reconstruct the social so as to further the capabilities of individual and social actors', the "capability-pragmatist" catch phrase might be articulated. There are no absolute formulas as to how this should be done, but instead one can assess the furthering of capabilities on a case-by-case basis. However, this experimentation should not be done by relying purely on trial and error but with a clear understanding of the issues involved and with comprehensive plans. Dewey was, however, too reliant on local communal life as a source of the public (Whipple 2005). In a globalized world, Mead's vision of a "universalized other" also needs non-local and even global publics. In a conflict-ridden world, an inclusive generalized other is a regulative ideal definitely worth striving for.

CHAPTER 6

The Road Ahead

While speaking of the preferable rhetoric of pragmatists, Rorty (1999, xix) argued that "our efforts at persuasion must take the form of gradual inculcation of new ways of speaking, rather than of straightforward argument with old ways of speaking." I, for one, prefer straightforward argumentation rather than inculcation. Nor do I think that pragmatism would imply a wholly new way of speaking. At least in the field of social theory, pragmatist themes are familiar from previous discussions within this field. However, *the perspective* is somewhat novel. The main argument that I have put forward is that action and the phenomenon of habituality are essential in explaining social reproduction. Habituality is not the only key to such explanations but it is a key nevertheless – and one that has not been taken into account as much as it should be. Habits are bodily and therefore it can seem that they are a purely individual phenomenon. However, due to the intersubjective nature of human sociality, we almost instinctively take the habitual attitudes of others into account and adjust our own action accordingly.

As previously discussed, the concept of habit has also been present in social theory in other contexts besides the pragmatist one. What I have tried to show is that in the pragmatist framework it is the main concept, not a residual category of some other phenomenon. This order of things allows one to develop a naturalist, action-centered theory of social structures – a theory which does not downplay the role of reflexivity but allocates it to a phase of action processes. Reflexive pondering, with the help of mental and social representations, is especially present in situations where habits and their environments are in conflict. Such situations are certainly plentiful. Conceptually one can say that habits *mediate* action and social structures. Thus, habits are not the same thing as action or structure, but such action which is habitual tends to (re)produce social structures. This stance allows one to combat, among other things, an excessive emphasis on discursive factors which has undoubtedly been a common feature of sociology in recent years (for example, in the form of social constructionism).

A pragmatist answer to the constructionist claim would be something like this: Yes, knowledge is often socially constructed but no, this does not mean that knowledge would always be purely arbitrary. Knowing is a part or a phase of action, not something external to it. Constructionism also sometimes contains – explicitly or implicitly – conclusions which are too pessimistic regarding the very possibility of knowing. Haack (2008, 26) has labeled these pessimistic views "New Cynicism." Such views share "a profound intolerance of uncertainty and a deep unwillingness to accept that the less than perfect is a lot better than nothing at all" (ibid.). What Haack is driving at is that knowing is certainly an untidy process – and very often we do not get things right. However, this is no reason for despair. What it does mean is that one should be a fallibilist, that is, open to evidence and willing to change one's beliefs in the face of such evidence. One could also add that, yes, our ways of classifying things can have effects on the very things being classified. On the other hand, this mainly concerns those things that Hacking (1999) has called interactive kinds. This concept refers mainly to classifications of human beings since humans can become aware of the ways that they are classified. However, there are also *indifferent kinds* which refer to those classes of phenomena that do not interact with our classifications. The lesson to be learned is that reality has an independent "push" and getting sense of this push, although an active process on our part, is not a matter of wishful thinking. In addition, rather than postulating a cultural monolith that constructs us through language, it is useful to see that "[c]ulture appears to be a conceptual resource that individuals draw on selectively (in a context-sensitive and task-specific manner) and in a filtered form (subject to a vast suite of innate human cognitive constraints)" (Slingerland 2008, 106).

Pragmatism has always been a moderate philosophy in relation to social reforms. Reform, on the basis of existing habits, rather than revolution, is its credo. This moderate stance is one of the important features of pragmatism in other respects as well. For example, in relation to evolutionary theory one can say that it has relevance for social sciences but its relevance mainly directs our attention towards a more action-centered approach than has sometimes been common. There is also the possibility of analogical usage of evolutionary theory in explaining the variation of institutions. Thus, no reductive attitudes are implied by evolutionary theory in the pragmatist context. However, sociology should not evade seeing what neighboring disciplines are up to. The behavioral sciences are advancing with major leaps and the social sciences can learn many lessons from these advances.

My discussion has been on a fairly abstract level but I see no reasons why one could not use these conceptual ideas as guides for empirical research as well. Of course, such guidance cannot be mechanical and therefore more concrete operationalizations of these concepts are called for in the future. Thus, one of the open questions left for future research has to do with the relationship with empirical research, especially with the possible operationalizations of the concept of habit. All research also faces the question of its possible larger societal relevance. This question, although a complex one, is certainly in order in the case of theoretical research as well. So does my research have some relevance besides contributions which can attract interest from social scientists? The answer is in the affirmative. Some of this relevance is already spelled out in previous chapters but here I will present some very general outlines.

At least since the 1980s the Western political climate has been such that it favors a view in which actors are seen as calculators of their interests – and more or less disconnected from the social setting and from history. A related presupposition is the belief that "work is irksome," as Veblen (1898, 187) diagnosed in his time; work is thus naturally disagreeable to human beings, who find satisfaction only in a state of passivity. One can say with near certainty that this view is false. Choosing among different options is a part of everyday life, and incentives can have bearing on this issue, but all operations of choice take place in a scene set by our social relations and existing habits. What we, and those that we deem important, have previously been doing is thus an important factor in explaining our present lines of conduct. A major part of such previous conduct is the physical and social environment in which this conduct has taken place. The habitual nature of action also implies that "it's easier to change our environment than our mind," as Wansink (2006, 25) states in a discussion on food-related habits.

To conclude I would like to refer once again to Bernstein (1992, 832) and argue that the spirit of pragmatism "has been (*pace* Rorty) *not* deconstruction but reconstruction." Pragmatism emphasizes the grounding of our conceptions in specific and concrete cultural settings. These settings are something that cannot be avoided, whether we like it or not. However, as Bernstein clarifies, and contrary to Rorty's claims, pragmatism is not limited to specific contexts because pragmatism also "endeavors to *transcend* the limitations of context" (ibid., 834). Thus, we are always, to some extent, at the mercy of our particular habits – but at the same time the regulative ideal should be a critical community of enquirers. And to argue along Bourdieusian/Meadian lines, a society which is sharply divided by class-based habits is a society where people can take the attitudes of others into account but often in a negative manner, as something to oppose or to sneer at. Such a society can find it difficult to realize the Deweyan ideal of democracy as the very idea of community life because any agreement on the problems, that is, on the nature of public, can be hard to come by. However, the road ahead is not necessarily bleak because our multiple and overlapping identities, embedded in our habits, potentially enable generalizing and seeing things from a larger perspective.

References

Aboulafia, Mitchell (1999): A (neo) American in Paris: Bourdieu, Mead, and Pragmatism. In Shusterman, Richard (ed.), 153-174.
Aboulafia, Mitchell (2001): *The Cosmopolitan Self. George Herbert Mead and Continental Philosophy*. Urbana and Chicago: University of Illinois Press.
Aboulafia, Mitchell (2006): Expressivism and Mead's Social Self. In J. R. Shook & J. Margolis (eds.): *A Companion to Pragmatism*. Malden, MA: Blackwell, 193-201.
Aldrich, Howard E., Geoffrey M. Hodgson, David L. Hull, Thorbjorn Knudsen, Joel Mokyr & Viktor J. Vanberg (2008): In Defence of Generalized Darwinism. *Journal of Evolutionary Economics* 18:5, 577-596.
Aranson, Peter H. (1998): The New Institutional Analysis of Politics. *Journal of Institutional and Theoretical Economics* 154:4 744-753.
Archer, Margaret S. (1988): *Culture and Agency. The Place of Culture in Social Theory*. Cambridge: Cambridge University Press.
Archer, Margaret S. (2000): *Being Human. The Problem of Agency*. Cambridge: Cambridge University Press.
Archer, Margaret S. (2002): Realism and the Problem of Agency. *Journal of Critical Realism* 5:1, 11-20.
Archer, Margaret S. (2003): *Structure, Agency and the Internal Conversation*. Cambridge: Cambridge University Press.
Archer, Margaret S. (2007): *Making Our Way through the World. Human Reflexivity and Social Mobility*. Cambridge: Cambridge University Press.
Archer, Margaret & Jonathan Q. Tritter (eds.) (2000): *Rational Choice Theory. Resisting Colonization*. London and New York: Routledge.
Baert, Patrick & Bryan S. Turner (2007): Introduction. In Baert, Patrick & Turner, Bryan S. (eds.): *Pragmatism and European Social Theory*. Oxford: Bardwell Press.
Baldwin, John D. (1988): The Matter of Habit and G. H. Mead: Comment on Camic. *American Journal of Sociology* 93:4, 952-957.

Baldwin, John D. (2002): *George Herbert Mead. A Unifying Theory for Sociology.* Dubuque: Kendall/Hunt.
Bargh, John A. & Tanya L. Chartrand (1999): The Unbearable Automacity of Being. *American Psychologist* 54:7, 462-479.
Baron-Cohen, Simon (1995): *Mindblindness: An Essay on Autism and Theory of Mind.* Cambridge & London: The MIT Press.
Beck, Ulrich & Elisabeth Beck-Gernheim (2002): *Individualization. Institutionalized Individualism and its Social and Political Consequences.* London: Sage.
Beckert, Jens (2002): *Beyond the Market. The Social Foundations of Efficiency.* Princeton and Oxford: Princeton University Press.
Beckert, Jens (2003). Economic Sociology and Embeddedness: How Shall We Conceptualize Economic Action? *Journal of Economic Issues* 37:3, 769-787.
Berger, Peter L. & Thomas Luckmann ([1966] 1995), *The Social Construction of Reality. A Treatise in the Sociology of Knowledge*, Harmondsworth: Penguin Books.
Bergman, Mats (2004): *Fields of Signification. Explorations in Charles S. Peirce's Theory of Signs.* Philosophical Studies from the University of Helsinki 6.
Bernstein, Richard J. (1983): *Beyond Objectivism and Relativism. Science, Hermeneutics, and Praxis.* Philadelphia: University of Pennsylvania Press.
Bernstein, Richard J. (1987): One Step Forward, Two Steps Backward. Richard Rorty on Liberal Democracy and Philosophy. *Political Theory* 15:4, 583-563.
Bernstein, Richard J. (1992): The Resurgence of Pragmatism. *Social Research* 59:4, 813-840.
Bertilsson, Thora Margareta (2009): *Peirce's Theory of Inquiry and Beyond. Towards a Social Reconstruction of Science Theory.* Frankfurt am Main: Peter Lang.
Bogdan, Radu J. (1994): *Grounds for Cognition. How Goal-Guided Behavior Shapes the Mind.* Hillsdale: Lawrence Erlbaum.
Bogdan, Radu J. (2003): *Minding Minds. Evolving a Reflexive Mind by Interpreting Others.* Cambridge and London: The MIT Press.
Bohman, James (1999): Practical Reason and Cultural Constraint: Agency in Bourdieu's Theory of Practice. In Richard Shusterman (ed.) (1999), 129-152.
Bohman, James (2010): Participation through Publics: Did Dewey answer Lippmann? *Contemporary Pragmatism* 7:1, 49-68.
Bourdieu, Pierre (1977): *Outline of a Theory of Practice.* Cambridge: Cambridge University Press.
Bourdieu, Pierre (1984): *Distinction. A Social Critique of the Judgement of Taste.* New York & London: Routledge.
Bourdieu, Pierre (1990a): *The Logic of Practice.* Stanford: Stanford University Press.
Bourdieu, Pierre (1990b): *In Other Words. Essays Towards a Reflexive Sociology.* Stanford: Stanford University Press.
Bourdieu, Pierre (1991): *Language and Symbolic Power.* Cambridge: Polity Press.
Bourdieu, Pierre (1998): *Practical Reason. On the Theory of Action.* Stanford: Stanford University Press.
Bourdieu, Pierre (2000): *Pascalian Meditations.* Stanford: Stanford University Press.
Bourdieu, Pierre (2005): *The Social Structures of the Economy.* Cambridge: Polity Press.

References

Bourdieu, Pierre & Loïc J. D. Wacquant (1992): *An Invitation to Reflexive Sociology*. Cambridge and Oxford: Polity Press.
Brette, Olivier (2003): Thorstein Veblen's Theory of Institutional Change: Beyond Technological Determinism. *European Journal of the History of Economic Thought* 10:3, 455-477.
Brinton, Mary C. & Victor Nee (eds.) (1998): *The New Institutionalism in Sociology*. New York: Russell Sage Foundation.
Brubaker, Rogers (1993): Social Theory as Habitus. In Craig Calhoun , LiPuma, Edward & Postone, Moishe (ed.), 212-234.
Calhoun, Craig, Edward LiPuma & Moishe Postone (eds.) (1993): *Bourdieu: Critical Perspectives*. Cambridge and Oxford: Polity Press.
Camic, Charles (1986): The Matter of Habit. *American Journal of Sociology* 91:5, 1039-1087.
Camic, Charles (1987): The Making of a Method: A Historical Reinterpretation of the Early Parsons. *American Sociological Review* 52:4 421-439.
Camic, Charles (1988): Reply to Baldwin. *American Journal of Sociology* 93:4, 957-958.
Campbell, Colin (1995): The Myth of Social Action. Cambridge: Cambridge University Press.
Campbell, James (1998): Dewey's Conception of Community. In Hickman, Larry A. (ed.): *Reading Dewey. Interpretations for a Postmodern Generation*. Bloomington & Indianapolis: Indiana University Press.
Clark, Andy (1999): An Embodied Cognitive Science? *Trends in Cognitive Sciences* 3:9, 345-351.
Claxton, Guy (2005): *The Wayward Mind. An Intimate History of the Unconscious*. London: Abacus.
Colapietro, Vincent (2004a): Doing – and Undoing – the Done Thing: Dewey and Bourdieu on Habituation, Agency, and Transformation. *Contemporary Pragmatism* 1:2, 65-93.
Colapietro, Vincent (2004b): Toward a Truly Pragmatic Theory of Signs. Reading Peirce's Semeiotic in Light of Dewey's Gloss. In E. L. Khalil (ed.): *Dewey, Pragmatism, and Economic Methodology*. London and New York: Routledge, 102-129.
Cook, Gary A. (1993): *George Herbert Mead. The Making of a Social Pragmatist*. Urbana and Chicago: University of Illinois Press.
Cook, Gary A. (2006): George Herbert Mead. In Shook, John R & Margolis Joseph (eds.): *A Companion to Pragmatism*. Malden, MA: Blackwell, 67-78.
Cooley, Charles ([1909] 1956): *Human Nature and the Social Order*. Revised Edition. Clencoe: The Free Press.
Damasio, Antonio (2000): *The Feeling of What Happens. Body, Emotion and the Making of Consciousness*. London: Vintage.
da Silva, Filipa Carreira (2006): G. H. Mead in the History of Sociological Ideas. *Journal of the History of the Behavioral Sciences* 42:1, 19-39.
Deacon, Terrence (1997): *The Symbolic Species. The Co-evolution of Language and the Brain*. New York: Norton.
Dennett, Daniel (1995): *Darwin's Dangerous Idea. Evolution and the Meanings of Life*. London: Penguin.
Dennett, Daniel (1996): *Kinds of Minds. The Origins of Consciousness*. London: Phoenix.
Denzau, Arthut T. & Douglass C. North (1994): Shared Mental Models: Ideologies and Institutions. *Kyklos* 47:1, 3-31.

Dewey, John (1910): *The Influence of Darwin on Philosophy. And Other Essays in Contemporary Thought*. New York: Henry Holt.
Dewey, John (1927): *The Public and its Problems*. New York: Henry Holt and Company.
Dewey, John ([1910] 1997): *How We Think*. New York: Dover.
Dewey, John ([1922] 2002): *Human Nature and Conduct*. New York: Dover.
Dewey, John & Arthur F. Bentley (1949): *Knowing and the Known*. Boston: Beacon Press.
DiMaggio, Paul J. and Walter W. Powell (1991): Introduction. In Walter W. Powell and Paul J. DiMaggio (eds.): *The New Institutionalism in Organizational Analysis*. Chicago and London: University of Chicago Press: 1-38.
Durkheim, Emile (1933): *The Division of Labor in Society*. Glencoe: The Free Press.
Durkheim, Émile ([1955] 1983): *Pragmatism and Sociology*. Edited and introduced by John B. Allcock. Cambridge: Cambridge University Press.
Eggertsson, Thráinn (1990): *Economic Behavior and Institutions*. Cambridge: Cambridge University Press.
Elder-Vass, Dave (2007): Reconciling Archer and Bourdieu in an Emergentist Theory of Action. *Sociological Theory* 25:4, 325-346.
Ensminger, Jean (1998): Anthropology and the New Institutionalism. *Journal of Institutional and Theoretical Economics* 154:4, 774-789.
Feldman, Martha S. & Brian T. Pentland (2003): Reconceptualizing Organizational Routines as a Source of Flexibility and Change. *Administrative Science Quarterly* 48:1, 94-118.
Field, Alexander James (1981): The Problem with Neoclassical Institutional Economics: A Critique with Special Reference to the North/Thomas Model of Pre-1500 Europe. *Explorations in Economic History* 18:2, 174-198.
Fleetwood, Steve (2008): Institutions and Social Structures. *Journal for the Theory of Social Behaviour* 38:3, 241-265.
Fontana, Andrea, Rick Tilman, & Linda Roe (1992): Theoretical Parallels in George H. Mead and Thorstein Veblen. *Social Science Journal* 29:3, 241-259.
Frangie, Samer (2009): Bourdieu's Reflexive Politics: Socio-Analysis, Biography and Self-Creation. *European Journal of Social Theory* 12:2, 213-229.
Franks, David D. (2010): *Neurosociology. The Nexus between Neuroscience and Social Psychology*. New York: Springer.
Gallese, Vittorio (2006): Intentional Attunement: A Neurophysiological Perspective on Social Cognition and its Disruption in Autism. *Brain Research* 1079, 15-24.
Gärdenfors, Peter (2003): *How Homo Became Sapiens. On the Evolution of Thinking*. Oxford: Oxford University Press.
Giddens, Anthony (1986): *The Constitution of Society. Outline of the Theory of Structuration*. Cambridge: Polity Press.
Gillespie, Alex (2005): G. H. Mead: Theorist of the Social Act. *Journal for the Theory of Social Behavior* 35:1, 19-39.
Gladwell, Malcolm (2005): *Blink. The Power of Thinking without Thinking*. London: Penguin.
Gladwell, Malcolm (2008): *Outliers. The Story of Success*. New York: Little, Brown and Company.
Granovetter, Mark (1985): Economic Action and Social Structure: The Problem of Embeddedness. *American Journal of Sociology* 91:3, 481-510.

References

Greif, Avnir (2006): *Institutions and the Path to the Modern Economy. Lessons from Medieval Trade.* New York: Cambridge University Press.

Gronow, Antti (2008a): The Over- or the Undersocialized Conception of Man? Practice Theory and the Problem of Intersubjectivity *Sociology* 42:2, 243-259.

Gronow, Antti (2008b): Not by Rules or Choice Alone: A Pragmatist Critique of Institution Theories in Economics and Sociology. *Journal of Institutional Economics* 4:3, 351-373.

Gronow, Jukka (1997): *The Sociology of Taste*. London and New York: Routledge.

Gross, Neil (2002): Becoming a Pragmatist Philosopher: Status, Self-Concept, and Intellectual Choice. *American Sociological Review* 67:4, 52-76.

Gross, Neil (2009): A Pragmatist Theory of Social Mechanisms. *American Sociological Review* 74:3, 358-379).

Haack, Susan (1993): *Evidence and Inquiry. Towards Recostruction in Epistemology.* Oxford and Malden, MA: Blackwell.

Haack, Susan (2004): Pragmatism, Old and New. *Contemporary Pragmatism* 1:1, 3-41.

Haack, Susan (2007): *Defending Science – Within Reason. Between Scientism and Cynicism.* New York: Prometheus Books.

Haack, Susan (2008): *Putting Philosophy to Work. Inquiry and its Place in Culture.* New York: Prometheus Books.

Hacking, Ian (1999): *The Social Construction of What?* Cambridge & London: Harvard University Press.

Hall, Stuart (2001): Foucault: Power, Knowledge and Discourse. In Whetherell, Margaret, Taylor, Stephanie & Yates, Simeon J. (eds.): *Discourse Theory and Practice. A Reader.* London: Sage, 72-81.

Heiskala, Risto (2003): *Society as Semiosis. Neostructuralist Theory of Culture and Society.* Frakfurt am Main: Peter Lang.

Heiskala, Risto (2007): Economy and Society. From Parsons through Habermas to Semiotic Institutionalism. *Social Science Information* 46:2, 243-272.

Heritage, John (1984): *Garfinkel and Ethnomethodology.* Cambridge: Polity Press.

Hildebrand, David L. (2008): *Dewey. A Beginners Guide.* Oxford: Oneworld.

Hodgson, Geoffrey M. (2001): *How Economics Forgot History. The Problem of Historical Specifity in Social Science.* London and New York: Routledge.

Hodgson, Geoffrey M. (2004): *The Evolution of Institutional Economics: Agency, Structure and Darwinism in American Institutionalism.* London and New York: Routledge.

Hodgson, Geoffrey M. (2006): *Economics in the Shadow of Darwin and Marx. Essays on Institutional and Evolutionary Themes.* Cheltenham & Northampton, MA: Edward Elgar.

Hodgson, Geoffrey M. (2007): Meanings of Methodological Individualism. *Journal of Economic Methodology* 14:2, 211-226.

Hodgson, Geoffrey M. (2010): Darwinian Coevolution of Organizations and the Environment. *Ecological Economics* 69:4, 700-706.

Hodgson, Geoffrey M. and Thorbjorn Knudsen (2006): Why We Need a Generalized Darwinism, and Why Generalized Darwinism is Not Enough. *Journal of Economic Behavior and Organization* 61:1, 1-19.

Hutchins, Edwin (2006): The Distributed Cognition Perspective on Human Interaction. Teoksessa Enfield, N. J. & Levinson, Stephen C. (toim.): *Roots of Human Sociality. Culture, Cognition and Interaction.* Oxford & New York: Berg, 375-398.

Iacoboni, Marco (2008): *Mirroring People. The New Science of How We Connect with Others.* New York: Farrar, Straus & Giroux.
Jablonka, Eva & Marion J. Lamb (2005): *Evolution in Four Dimensions. Genetic, Epigenetic, Behavioral, and Symbolic Variation in the History of Life.* Cambridge & London: The MIT Press.
James, William ([1907] 1975): *Pragmatism. A New Name for Some Old Ways of Thinking.* Contains also *The Meaning of Truth: A Sequel to Pragmatism* [1909]. Cambridge and London: Harvard University Press.
Jenkins, Richard (2002): *Pierre Bourdieu.* Revised Edition. London & New York: Routldege.
Joas, Hans (1985): *G. H. Mead. A Contemporary Re-examination of his Thought.* Cambridge: Polity Press.
Joas, Hans (1993): *Pragmatism and Social Theory.* Chicago & London: University of Chicago Press.
Joas, Hans (1996): *The Creativity of Action.* Cambridge: Polity Press.
Joas, Hans (2008): *Do We Need Religion? On the Experience of Self-Transcendence.* Boulder & London: Paradigm Publishers.
Joas, Hans & Erkki Kilpinen (2006): Creativity and Society. In John R. Shook & Joseph Margolis (eds.): *A Companion to Pragmatism.* Malden, MA: Blackwell, 323-335.
Joas, Hans & Knöbl, Wolfgang (2009): *Social Theory. Twenty Introductory Lectures.* New York: Cambridge University Press.
Johnson, Mark (2006): Cognitive Science. In In Shook, John R. & Margolis, Joseph (eds.): *A Companion to Pragmatism.* Malden, MA: Blackwell, 369-377.
Johnson, Mark (2007): *The Meaning of the Body: Aesthetics of Human Understanding.* Chicago & London: University of Chicago Press.
Ketokivi, Kaisa (2008): The Biographical Disruption, the Wounded Self and the Reconfiguration of Significant Others. In Widmer, Eric & Jallinoja, Riitta (eds.): *Beyond the Nuclear Family: Families in a Configurational Perspective.* Bern: Peter Lang, 255-277.
Khalil, Elias L. (2004): Introduction: John Dewey, the Transactional View and the Behavioral Sciences. In Elias L. Khalil (ed.): *Dewey, Pragmatism, and Economic Methodology.* London and New York: Routledge, 1-12.
Kilpinen, Erkki (2000): *The Enormous Fly-Wheel of Society. Pragmatism's Habitual Conception of Action and Social Theory.* University of Helsinki: Department of Sociology. Research Reports No. 235.
Kilpinen, Erkki (2003): Does Pragmatism Imply Institutionalism? *Journal of Economic Issues.* 37:2 291-304.
Kilpinen, Erkki (2004): How to Fight the "Methodenstreit"? Veblen and Weber on Economics, Psychology and Action. *International Review of Sociology* 14:3, 413-432.
Kilpinen, Erkki (2008): Memes Versus Signs: On the Use of Meaning Concepts About Nature and Culture. *Semiotica* 171 (1/4), 215-237.
Kilpinen, Erkki (2009a): The Habitual Conception of Action and Social Theory. *Semiotica* 173 (1/4), 99-128.
Kilpinen, Erkki (2009b): Pragmatism as a Philosophy of Action. In Pihlström, Sami & Rydenfelt, Henrik (eds.): *Pragmatist Perspectives.* Helsinki: Acta Philosophica Fennica vol. 86.

References

Kilpinen, Erkki (forthcoming): Social Theory. In Pihlström, Sami (ed.): *The Continuum Companion to Pragmatism.* New York & London: Continuum (the references are to the page numbers of the manuscript).

Kivinen, Osmo & Tero Piiroinen (2006): Toward Pragmatist Methodological Relationalism. From Philosophizing Sociology to Sociologizing Philosophy. *Philosophy of the Social Sciences* 36:3, 303-329.

Kloppenberg, James T. (1996): Pragmatism: An Old Name for Some New Ways of Thinking? *Journal of American History* 83:1, 100-138.

Kloppenberg, James T. (2011): *Reading Obama. Dreams, Hope, and the American Political Tradition.* Princeton: Princeton University Press.

Konrath, Sara H., Edward H. O'Brien & Courtney Hsing (2010): Changes in Dispositional Empathy in American College Students Over Time: A Meta-Analysis. *Personality and Social Psychology Review* Published online 5 August 2010.

Lakoff, George & Mark Johnson (1980): *Metaphors We Live By.* Chicago and London: University of Chicago Press.

Lakoff, George & Mark Johnson (1999): *Philosophy in the Flesh. The Embodied Mind and its Challenge to Western Thought.* New York: Basic Books.

Lebaron, Frédéric (2003): Pierre Bourdieu: Economic Models Against Economism. *Theory and Society* 32:5-6, 551-565.

Liebhafsky, E. E. (1993): The Influence of Charles Sanders Peirce on Institutional Economics. *Journal of Economic Issues* 27:3, 741-754.

Luhtakallio, Eeva (2010): *Local Politicizations. A Comparison of Finns and French Practicing Democracy.* University of Helsinki: Department of Social Research, Sociology Research Raports no. 265.

Lyng, Stephen & Franks, David D. (2002): *Sociology and the Real World.* Lanham: Rowman & Littlefield.

Määttänen, Pentti (2009): *Toiminta ja kokemus. Pragmatistista terveen järjen filosofiaa* [Action and Experience. Pragmatist Philosophy of Common Sense]. Helsinki: Gaudeamus (in Finnish).

MacGilvaray, Eric (2010): Dewey's Public. *Contemporary Pragmatism* 7:1, 31-47.

Macy, Michael W. (1997): Identity, Interest and Emergent Rationality: An Evolutionary Synthesis. *Rationality and Society* 9:4, 427-448.

Margolis, Joseph (2006): Introduction: Pragmatism, Retrospective and Prospective. In Shook, John R & Margolis Joseph (eds.): *A Companion to Pragmatism.* Malden, MA: Blackwell, 1-10.

McCormick, Ken (2006): *Veblen in Plain English. A Complete Introduction to Thorstein Veblen's Economics.* New York: Cambria Press.

Mead, George Herbert (1922): A Behavioristic Account of the Significant Symbol. In Mead (1964), 240-247.

Mead, George Herbert (1925): The Genesis of the Self and Social Control. In Mead (1964), 267-293.

Mead, George Herbert (1936): *Movements of Thought in the Nineteenth Century.* Chicago and Illinois: University of Chicago Press.

Mead, George Herbert (1964): *Selected Writings.* Edited by A. J. Reck. Indianapolis: Bobbs-Merril.

Mead, George Herbert ([1934] 1967): *Mind, Self, and Society. From the Standpoint of a Social Behaviorist*. Chicago: University of Chicago Press.

Meyer, John W. & Brian Rowan (1991): Institutionalized Organizations: Formal Structure as Myth and Ceremony. In Walter W. Powell & Paul J DiMaggio (eds.): *The New Institutionalism in Organizational Analysis*, Chicago and London: University of Chicago Press, 41-62.

Misak, Cheryl (2000): *Truth, Politics, Morality. Pragmatism and Deliberation*. London & New York: Routledge.

Misak, Cheryl (2007): Introduction. In Misak, Cheryl (ed.): *New Pragmatism*. Oxford: Clarendon Press, 1-6.

Mutch, Alistair (2004): Constraints on the Internal Conversation: Margaret Archer and the Structural Shaping of Thought. *Journal for the Theory of Social Behaviour* 34:4, 429-445.

Nee, Victor (1998): The Sources of the New Institutionalism. In Mary C. Brinton & Victor Nee (eds.): *The New Institutionalism in Sociology*. New York: Russel Sage Foundation, 1-16.

Nee, Victor & Paul Ingram (1998): Embeddedness and Beyond: Institutions, Exchange, and Social Structure. In Mary C. Brinton & Victor Nee (eds.): *The New Institutionalism in Sociology*. New York: Russel Sage Foundation, 19-45.

Nihtilä, Elina & Pekka Martikainen (2008): Institutionalization of Older Adults After the Death of a Spouse. *American Journal of Public Health* 98:7, 1228-1234.

Noë, Alva (2004): *Action in Perception*. Cambridge and London: The MIT Press.

Noë, Alva (2009): *Out of Our Heads. Why You are Not Your Brain, and Other Lessons from the Biology of Consciousness*. New York: Hill and Wang.

North, Douglass C. (1990): *Institutions, Institutional Change and Economic Performance*. Cambridge, Cambridge University Press.

Nussbaum, Martha (2000): *Women and Human Development. The Capabilities Approach*. Cambridge: Cambridge University Press.

Nussbaum, Martha & Amartya Sen (eds.) (1993): *The Quality of Life*, Clarendon Press, Oxford.

Ostrow, James M. (1990): *Social Sensitivity. A Study of Habit and Experience*. Albany: State University of New York.

Parsons, Talcott ([1937] 1949): *The Structure of Social Action. A Study in Social Theory with Special Reference to a Group of Recent European Writers*. New York: The Free Press of Glencoe.

Peirce, Charles S. (1931-1958): *Collected Papers of Charles Sanders Peirce*. 8 volumes. Edited by C. Hartshorne, P. Weiss and A. W. Burks. Cambridge MA: Harvard University Press.

Peirce, Charles S. ([1894] 1998): What is a Sign? In *The Essential Peirce, Volume 2 (1893-1913)*. Edited by The Peirce Edition Project. Bloomington and Indianapolis: Indiana University Press, 4-10.

Perraton, Jonathan and Iona Tarrant (2007): What Does Tacit Knowledge Actually Explain? *Journal of Economic Methodology* 14:3, 353-370.

Plotkin, Henry (2003): *The Imagined World Made Real. Towards a Natural Science of Culture*. New Brunswick: Rutgers University Press.

Polanyi, Karl ([1944] 2001): *The Great Transformation. The Political and Economic Origins of Our Time*. Boston: Beacon Press.

Popp, Jerome A. (2007): *Evolution's First Philosopher. John Dewey and the Continuity of Nature*. Albany: State University of New York.
Purhonen, Semi, Jukka Gronow & Keijo Rahkonen (2009): Social Differentiation of Musical and Literary Taste Patterns in Finland. *Research on Finnish Society* Vol. 2, 39-49.
Quellette, Judith A. & Wendy Wood (1998): Habit and Intention in Everyday Life: The Multiple Processes by Which Past Behavior Predicts Future Behavior. *Psychological Bulletin* 124:1, 54-74.
Rahkonen, Keijo (1999): *Not Class but Struggle. Critical Ouvertures to Pierre Bourdieu's Sociology*. University of Helsinki: Department of Social Policy Research Reports 1/1999.
Reckwitz, Andrew (2002): Toward a Theory of Social Practices. A Development in Culturalist Theorizing. *European Journal of Social Theory* 5:2, 243-263.
Rescher, Nicholas (2008): Process Philosophy. In the *Stanford Encyclopedia of Philosophy*. Published online: http://plato.stanford.edu/entries/process-philosophy (accessed 16/12/2009).
Richerson, Peter J. & Robert Boyd (2005): *Not By Genes Alone. How Culture Transformed Human Evolution*. Chicago: University of Chicago Press.
Ridley, Matt (2004): *Nature via Nurture. Genes, Experience and What Makes Us Human*. London: Harper Perennial.
Rizza, Robert (2006): The Relationship between Economics and Sociology: The Contribution of Economic Sociology, Setting out from the Problem of Embeddedness. *International Review of Sociology* 16:1, 31-48.
Robeyns, Ingrid (2005): The Capability Approach: A Theoretical Survey. *Journal of Human Development* 6:1, 93-114.
Rochberg-Halton, Eugene (1986): *Meaning and Modernity. Social Theory in the Pragmatic Attitude*. Chicago and London: University of Chicago Press.
Rorty, Richard (1999): *Philosophy and Social Hope*. London: Penguin Books.
Rorty, Richard (2007): Main Statement. In Rorty, Richard & Engel, Pascal: *What's the Use of Truth?* New York: Columbia University Press, 31-45.
Rutherford, Malcolm (1996): *Institutions in Economics. The Old and the New Institutionalism*. Cambridge: Cambridge University Press.
Sacks, Oliver (1995): *An Anthropologist on Mars. Seven Paradoxical Tales*. Basingstoke and Oxford: Picador.
Savidan, Patrick (2007): Introduction. In Rorty, Richard & Engel, Pascal: *What's the Use of Truth?* New York: Columbia University Press, ix-xii.
Sawyer, R. Keith (2001): Emergence in Sociology: Contemporary Philosophy of Mind and Some Implications for Sociological Theory. *American Journal of Sociology* 107:3, 551-585.
Schatzki, Theodore R., Karin Knorr Cetina & Eike von Savigny (eds.) (2001): *The Practice Turn in Contemporary Theory*. London and New York: Routledge.
Scott, W. Richard (2001): *Institutions and Organizations* (2nd Edition). Thousand Oaks: Sage.
Scott, W. Richard (2008): *Institutions and Organizations. Ideas and Interests*. Thousand Oaks: Sage.
Selznick, Philip (1966): *TVA and the Grass Roots. A Study in the Sociology of Formal Organization*. New York: Harper & Row.

Sen, Amartya (1985): Well-Being, Agency and Freedom. *Journal of Philosophy* 82:4, 169-221.
Sen, Amartya (1993): Capability and Well-Being. In Martha Nussbaum and Amartya Sen (1993), 30-53.
Sen, Amartya (2001): *Development as Freedom.* Oxford and New York: Oxford University Press.
Sen, Amartya (2010): *The Idea of Justice.* London: Penguin Books.
Shilling, Chris (1999): Towards an Embodied Understanding of the Structure/Agency Relationship. *British Journal of Sociology* 50:4, 543-562.
Shilling, Chris (2008): *Changing Bodies. Habit, Crisis and Creativity.* London: Sage.
Shusterman, Richard (ed.) (1999): *Bourdieu. A Critical Reader.* Oxford and Malden, MA: Blackwell.
Slingerland, Edward (2008): *What Science Offers the Humanities. Integrating Body and Culture.* Cambridge: Cambridge University Press.
Sperber, Dan (1996): *Explaining Culture. A Naturalistic Approach.* Oxford: Blackwell.
Sterelny, Kim (2003): *Thought in a Hostile World. The Evolution of Human Cognition.* Oxford: Blackwell.
Stones, Rob (2001): Refusing the Realism–Structuration Divide. *European Journal of Social Theory* 4:2, 177-197.
Sugden, Robert (1995): The Coexistence of Conventions. *Journal of Economic Behavior and Organization* 28:2, 241-256.
Sulkunen, Pekka (2009): *The Saturated Society. Regulating Lifestyles in Consumer Capitalism.* Thousand Oaks, CA: Sage.
Swartz, David (1997): *Culture and Power. The Sociology of Pierre Bourdieu.* Chicago and London: University of Chicago Press.
Swedberg, Richard & Mark Granovetter (2001): Introduction to the Second Edition. In Richard Swedberg & Mark Granovetter (eds.): *The Sociology of Economic Life* (2nd Edition). Boulder, CO: Westview Press, 1-28.
Sweetman, Paul (2003): Twenty-First Century Dis-ease? Habitual Reflexivity or the Reflexive Habitus. *Sociological Review* 51:4, 528-549.
Taylor, Charles (1993): To Follow a Rule…. In C. Calhoun, E. LiPuma and M. Postone (ed.), 45-60.
Taylor, Charles (1994): *Modern Social Imaginaries.* Duke & London: Duke University Press.
Tomasello, Michael (2008): *Origins of Human Communication.* Cambridge & London: The MIT Press.
Tomasello, Michael (2009): *Why We Cooperate.* Cambridge & London: The MIT Press.
Turner, Bryan S. (1991): Preface to the New Edition. In Talcott Parsons: *The Social System.* London: Routledge, xviii-xlv.
Turner, Stephen (1994): *The Social Theory of Practices. Tradition, Tacit Knowledge, and Presuppositions.* Cambridge: University of Chicago Press.
Turner, Stephen P. (2002): *Brains/Practices/Relativism. Social Theory after Cognitive Science.* Chicago and London: The University of Chicago Press.
Vandenberghe, Frédéric (2005): The Archers. A Tale of Folk (Final Episode?). *European Journal of Social Theory* 8:2, 227-237.
Veblen, Thorstein (1898): The Instinct of Workmanship and the Irksomeness of Labor. *American Journal of Sociology* 4:2, 187-201.

References

Veblen, Thorstein (1914): *The Instinct of Workmanship and the State of the Industrial Arts.* New York: Macmillan.

Veblen, Thorstein ([1919] 2002): *The Place of Science in Modern Civilization and Other Essays.* New Brunswick and London: Transaction Publishers.

Velthuis, Olav (1999): The Changing Relationship between Economic Sociology and Institutional Economics: From Talcott Parsons to Mark Granovetter. *American Journal of Economics and Sociology* 58:4, 629-649.

Wansink, Brian (2006): *Mindless Eating. Why We Eat More Than We Think.* London: Hay House.

Westbrook, Robert B. (1991): *John Dewey and American Democracy.* Cornell University Press, Ithaca and London.

Westbrook, Robert B. (2007): *Democratic Hope. Pragmatism and the Politics of Truth.* Ithaca and London: Cornell University Press.

Whipple, Mark (2005): The Dewey-Lippmann Debate Today: Communication Distortions, Reflective Agency, and Participatory Democracy. *Sociological Theory* 23:2, 156-178.

Whitford, Josh (2002): Pragmatism and the Untenable Dualism of Means and Ends: Why Rational Choice Theory Does Not Deserve Paradigmatic Privilege. *Theory and Society* 31:3, 325-363.

Wiley, Norbert (1994): *The Semiotic Self.* Cambridge: Polity Press.

Wilkinson, Richard & Kate Pickett (2010): *The Spirit Level. Why Equality is Better for Everyone* (published with revision). London: Penguin.

Williamson, Oliver E. (1985): *The Economic Institutions of Capitalism. Firms, Markets, Relational Contracting.* New York and London: The Free Press.

Wood, Wendy, Jeffrey M. Quinn, and Deborah A. Kashy (2002): Habits in Everyday Life: Thought, Emotion, and Action. *Journal of Personality and Social Psychology*, 83:6, 1281-1297.

Wrong, Dennis H. (1961): The Oversocialized Conception of Man in Modern Sociology. *American Sociological Review* 26:2, 183-193.

Wrong, Dennis H. (1999): *The Oversocialized Conception of Man.* New Bruswick and London: Transaction Publishers.

Ylikoski, Petri (2009): Pragmatismin maihinnousu [Pragmatism Has Landed]. *Tiede & edistys* 34:2, 166-169 (original in Finnish).

Zeuner, Lilli (1999): Margaret Archer on Structural and Cultural Morphogenesis. *Acta Sociologica* 42:1, 79-86.

Zimmermann, Bénédicte (2006): Pragmatism and the Capability Approach: Challenges in Social Theory and Empirical Research. *European Journal of Social Theory* 9:4, 467-484.

Index

Aboulafia, Mitchell 56, 76, 105, 112
Aldrich, Howard E. 49
Allen, Woody 41
Aranson, Peter H. 85
Archer, Margaret S. 12-13, 36, 41, 59, 70-74, 76, 78-82, 112, 117, 126

Baert, Patrick 13
Baldwin, John D. 32, 42
Bargh, John A. 31
Baron-Cohen, Simon 43, 77-78, 81
Beck, Ulrich 67
Beck-Gernsheim, Elisabeth 67
Beckert, Jens 87-88, 97, 101-102
Bentham, Jeremy 129
Bentley, Arthur 27-28, 35, 108
Berger, Peter L. 31, 69, 90-92, 96, 124, 126
Bergman, Mats 14
Bernstein, Richard J. 15-16, 19, 35, 122, 133
Bertilsson, Thora Margareta 29
Bhaskar, Roy 70
Blumer, Herbert 18, 37
Bohman, James 67
Bogdan, Radu J. 77, 81, 95-96
Bourdieu, Pierre 10, 12, 40, 47, 53-59, 72, 80, 95, 103-109, 111-119
Boyd, Robert 50
Brubaker, Rogers 104, 112

Calhoun, Craig 54, 103
Camic, Charles 32, 82, 96, 103, 108
Campbell, Colin 71

Campbell, James 65, 68
Chartrand, Tanya L. 31
Chomsky, Noam 40
Clark, Andy 26
Claxton, Guy 31
Colapietro, Vincent 56, 82, 105, 118
Cook, Gary A. 32, 35, 37, 63, 75-76
Cooley, Charles Horton 35, 42

Damasio, Antonio 81
Darwin, Charles 14, 22, 26, 92
Da Silva, Filipa Carreira 37
Deacon, Terrence 24, 40
Dennett, Daniel 22, 27-28
Denzau, Arthut T. 85
Dewey, John 9, 14, 17-20, 23, 27-28, 35, 42, 56, 60-61, 64-68, 78, 80, 84, 94-96, 104-105, 108-110, 112-115, 122, 125-130
DiMaggio, Paul J. 46, 89, 90, 92
Durkheim, Èmile 17-18, 32, 83, 87-88, 108

Eggertsson, Thráinn 86
Elder-Vass, Dave 111, 113

Feldman, Martha S. 94, 98
Field, Alexander James 87
Fleetwood, Steve 52
Fontana, Andrea 102
Foucault, Michel 47
Frangie, Samer 54, 59
Franks, David D. 25, 40, 44, 108, 125, 127
Freud, Sigmund 31, 40

Index

Gallese, Vittorio 44
Garfinkel, Harold 90
Giddens, Anthony 59, 70, 72, 89, 92, 124
Gillespie, Alex 16, 37
Gladwell, Malcolm 30
Granovetter, Mark 85, 90
Greif, Avnir 85, 101
Gronow, Antti 97, 99, 112, 124, 126
Gronow, Jukka 106
Gross, Neil 10, 17, 34, 41, 54-55, 58
Gärdenfors, Peter 72, 75

Haack, Susan 15, 29-30, 59, 97, 132
Habermas, Jürgen 37, 65
Hacking, Ian 39, 71, 132
Hall, Stuart 47
Hegel, Georg W. F. 14
Heiskala, Risto 41, 55, 73, 84, 91, 94, 101
Heritage, John 89
Hildebrand, David L. 25
Hitchcock, Alfred 39
Hodgson, Geoffrey M. 35, 45, 49-52, 70, 85, 87, 92-93, 97-98, 110
Husserl, Edmund 72
Hutchins, Edwin 28

Iacoboni, Marco 44
Ingram, Paul 86

Jablonka, Eva 50
James, William 14, 16, 20, 96
Jenkins, Richard 103, 106
Joas, Hans 9, 11-13, 17-20, 35, 37, 42, 56, 58, 74, 77, 79-80, 94-95, 97, 110-112
Johnson, Mark 21, 23, 31, 39, 53, 55, 101, 109

Ketokivi, Kaisa 16
Khalil, Elias L. 75
Kilpinen, Erkki 11, 13-14, 17, 20, 22, 24-25, 34-36, 75, 81, 92-94, 96-97, 108, 110-111, 124
Kivinen, Osmo 21, 29
Kloppenberg, James T. 9, 82, 97
Knöbl, Wolfgang 13, 18, 56, 58
Knudsen, Thorbjorn 49, 98
Konrath, Sara H. 57
Kuhn, Thomas 30

Lakoff, George 21, 39, 53, 55, 101, 109
Lamb, Marion J. 50

Lebaron, Frédéric 55
Liebhafsky, E. E. 94
Lippmann, Walter 64, 65
Luckmann, Thomas 31, 69, 90-92, 96, 124, 126
Luhmann, Niklas 49
Luhtakallio, Eeva 67
Lyng, Stephen 25, 40, 108, 125, 127

Määttänen, Pentti 23
MacGilvaray, Eric 67
Macy, Michael W. 47
Margolis, Joseph 14
Marshall, Alfred 88
Martikainen, Pekka 117, 118
Marx, Karl 66
McCormick, Ken 92
Mead, George Herbert 9, 14-15, 17-18, 27, 29, 35-44, 54, 56-57, 59, 63, 65-66, 68, 70-71, 74-77, 79, 81-82, 93, 99, 102, 104-105, 110, 112-113, 115-116, 119, 125-128, 130
Merton, Robert 89
Meyer, John W. 92
Misak, Cheryl 15-16, 29
Morgan, Conwy Lloyd 97
Morris, Charles 37
Mutch, Alistair 70

Nee, Victor 85-86
Nihtilä, Elina 117-118
Noë, Alva 31, 44, 112
North, Douglass C. 45, 85
Nussbaum, Martha C. 62, 121-122, 125

Obama, Barack 9
Ostrow, James M. 105

Pareto, Vilfredo 88
Park, Robert 18
Parsons, Talcott 13, 32, 86, 88-91, 93, 96, 98, 101, 124
Peirce, Charles S. 11, 14-15, 24, 29-30, 73-74, 79, 94
Pentland, Brian T. 94, 98
Perraton, Jonathan 100
Pickett, Kate 57
Pihlström, Sami 121
Piiroinen, Tero 21, 29
Plotkin, Henry 33
Polanyi, Karl 66, 90

Index

Popp, Jerome A. 14
Powell, Walter W. 46, 89, 90, 92
Purhonen, Semi 55

Quellette, Judith A. 94

Rahkonen, Keijo 55
Reckwitz, Andrew 36, 70, 92
Rescher, Nicholas 22
Richerson, Peter J. 50
Ridley, Matt 40, 50
Rizza, Robert 90
Robeyns, Ingrid 123, 128-129
Rochberg-Halton, Eugene 97
Rorty, Richard 10, 11, 15, 19-22, 24, 28, 35, 82, 97, 131, 133
Rydenfelt, Henrik 121

Sacks, Oliver 77, 82
Savidan, Patrick 22
Sayer, Andrew 70
Schatzki, Theodore R. 71
Scott, Richard W. 45-47, 83-84, 89-90, 96, 100
Selznick, Philip 88-89
Sen, Amartya 29, 57, 60-64, 66, 119, 121-126, 128-130
Shilling, Chris 12, 18, 28, 32-33, 70
Shusterman, Richard 54, 103
Slingerland, Edward 21, 31, 132
Smith, Adam 93
Sperber, Dan 51, 94, 98-99
Sterelny, Kim 26, 43, 63
Stones, Rob 70
Sugden, Robert 87
Sulkunen, Pekka 106
Swartz, David 54, 58, 103
Swedberg, Richard 85
Sweetman, Paul 55, 112

Tarrant, Iona 100, 108
Taylor, Charles 67
Thomas, William I. 18, 35
Tomasello, Michael 44, 52
Tritter, Jonathan Q. 71
Turner, Bryan S. 13, 88
Turner, Stephen 34, 73

Vandenberghe, Frédéric 70
Veblen, Thorstein 17, 28, 45, 62, 83, 92-98, 113, 133
Velthuis, Olav 88

Wacquant, Loïc J. D. 56-57, 105, 107, 114, 119
Wansink, Brian 133
Weber, Max 32, 50, 88, 108
Westbrook, Robert B. 19, 21, 23, 35, 64-66, 108, 129
Whipple, Mark 64, 129-130
Whitford, Josh 62, 95, 97
Wiley, Norbert 77
Wilkinson, Richard 57
Williamson, Oliver E. 85
Wood, Wendy 53, 94, 101
Wrong, Dennis H. 69

Ylikoski, Petri 15

Zeuner, Lilli 70
Zimmermann, Bénédicte 122
Znaniecki, Florian 18

Studies in Sociology:
Symbols, Theory and Society

Books Series

The series has been created by Elżbieta Hałas (Poland) and Risto Heiskala (Finland) in order to stimulate and develop cooperation in research on the meaning, forms and functions of symbolism in society. The series is open to various theoretical and methodological orientations in the studies of social symbolism. The aim of the series is to show the central place of the problems of symbolization and symbolism in sociology – processes of symbolization in everyday life, in collective actions, social movements, organizations, in the public sphere of institutions, as well as in the construction of collective memories and identities, in the construction of the state and the nation, in international relations and in globalization processes.

The series presents theoretical and empirical questions of symbolic power, symbolic hegemony, symbolic control and symbolic politics; integrating as well as transforming and liberating functions of social symbolism in the processes of interactions and communication which shape knowledge, values and social sentiments.

For submission of manuscripts or further information please contact the editors:

Elżbieta Hałas
Institute of Sociology
University of Warsaw
Karowa 18
00-927 Warsaw
Poland
ehalas@poczta.neostrada.pl
ehalas@uw.edu.pl

Risto Heiskala
Institute for Social Research, ISR
FIN-33014 University of Tampere
Finland
risto.heiskala@uta.fi

Studies in Sociology:
Symbols, Theory and Society

Edited by Elżbieta Hałas and Risto Heiskala

Vol. 1   Elżbieta Hałas (ed.): Symbols, Power and Politics. 2002.

Vol. 2   Risto Heiskala: Society as Semiosis. Neostructuralist Theory of Culture and Society. 2003.

Vol. 3   Jacob Alsted: A Model of Human Motivation for Sociology. 2005.

Vol. 4   Horst Jürgen Helle: Symbolic Interaction and *Verstehen*. 2005.

Vol. 5   Thora Margareta Bertilsson: Peirce's Theory of Inquiry and Beyond. Towards a Social Reconstruction of Science Theory. 2009.

Vol. 6   Elżbieta Hałas: Towards the World Culture Society. Florian Znaniecki's Culturalism. 2010.

Vol. 7   Antti Gronow: From Habits to Social Structures. Pragmatism and Contemporary Social Theory. 2011.

www.peterlang.de